Shrouds in the Snow
(The story of the New York City Park S

MW00457617

By Linda M. Boris

Illustrated by Louis Gonzalez

Author's Note

This book is a work of non-fiction. I have not embellished or added to the story beyond the accounts found in contemporaneous news stories, the report of the Civil Aviation Board's investigation into the disaster, journal articles written in commemoration of the 50th anniversary of the crash in 2010, and two eyewitness interviews. For those interviews, I am grateful to John Marrotta and Joseph DiFrulo for sharing their stories of their experience on the streets of Brooklyn after the crash of United 826 in the Park Slope neighborhood, where they both happened to be at the time of the tragedy. I am also grateful to Tim Azzara, and my illustrator, Louis Gonzalez—two aviation enthusiasts who have studied this particular aircraft crash for many years. I appreciate all the advice and insights they provided to me in the course of writing this book.

The vast majority of this work is taken from newspaper articles published at the time of the crash and the subsequent investigation. I cannot vouch for their accuracy or the accuracy of the eyewitness statements given to reporters at the time they were interviewed. In the heat of traumatic events, witnesses may perceive different things based on their own, sometimes flawed, recollections. Reporters, armed most likely with only a notepad and a stubby pencil, may mis-hear or misinterpret what they hear. Reporters, even though striving to be objective journalists, are human and see things through the filter of their own minds. So, perhaps, rather than a factually accurate and complete account of what happed on December 16, 1960 and the days that followed, this book attempts to place the reader at the scene—experiencing what the players in this story experienced and observed, be they crew, passengers, families, eye witnesses, first responders, or investigators. This is their story, as they lived it, as they perceived it. This is as close as we may be able to get to their reality. And their story deserves the telling.

---Linda Boris

Illustrator's Note

Growing up in Park Slope, I was always intrigued by the story of "the crash" recalled by my neighbors every December. As a child I thought it was an urban legend - far too devastating to be true. But one day, while driving by Sterling Place, my parents told me their account, and it was then that I realized that it was not just a tale. My mom told me how she heard what sounded like distant muffled thunder which shook the windows, and how some time later they walked over to the barricades and were struck by the vision of a burned and broken jetliner tail lying askew in the middle of the intersection. They also got a glimpse of a burned engine, perhaps as it was being carted away.

Like everyone else, I wondered: how could something like this possibly happen? I read everything that I could find, but there always seemed to be gaps in the information, and many things did not make sense. As the author points out, it is human nature to make errors when making eyewitness statements. My interest in aviation continued through college where I studied Aeronautical Engineering. This knowledge, combined with zealous study of the official accident report, finally led me to a better understanding of what happened that day, with regards to physics and engineering. I have tried to convey that in my illustrations, though they are still interpretations.

My heart goes out to all the humanity affected by this terrible disaster to this day. The accident led to many improvements in aviation. I am grateful to all the professionals who were directly involved and took great efforts to document and study this event.

---Louis Gonzalez

1

Johnny Marotta sat on a stoop on St. Mark's Avenue near his Brooklyn Heights home smoking a cigarette. Eighteen years old, a high school senior, he had decided to skip school today. The city had finally dug out of the early winter blizzard that had hit Sunday into Monday dumping up to seventeen inches of snow on New York and all of its boroughs. Schools had been closed or opened late almost all week. The temperatures had hit record lows. Now, Friday, December 16 was the first decent day since the storm hit. Temperatures climbed up into the high thirties and while it was cloudy, the sun managed to poke out now and then. As he sat there just watching cars go by, Johnny realized he was bored. All of his friends were either in school, where he should have been, or working. There was nothing to do but hang out and wait for them.

The Pepitones lived on St. Mark's Avenue. In a three-story tenement, Joey Pepitone, who was signed by the Yankees three years before, lived with his parents and other members of his extended family, including his uncle Jimmy. Johnny Marotta knew the family and considered Jimmy a friend. Around ten o'clock that morning, Jimmy happened by the stoop where Johnny was sitting. "Come on in and have a cup of coffee," Jimmy invited Johnny in. As they sat and drank their coffee, Jimmy asked, "What are you doing today?"

"I'm not doin' nothin'" Johnny replied.

"Well, I gotta go paint my mother's kitchen. You wanna give me a hand?"

"Sure," Johnny shrugged.

The two finished their coffee and headed out for the paint store in Jimmy's car. Pintchik's was the largest paint company in Brooklyn, located about twelve blocks away off Flatbush Avenue in the Park Slope section. It was the best place to buy paint in the area, so that's where they headed, taking Sterling Place, because that was the fastest way to get there. Cars lined both sides of the street and piles of dirty snow could be seen here and there against the curbs where the snow plows had dumped their loads. A large rental box truck, several car lengths in front of them blocked their view up Sterling. When they got near the intersection of Sterling and 7th, the box truck began to slow and then came to a stop at the stop sign. Jimmy pulled up behind the truck and waited for it to pass through the intersection, but it wasn't moving. He waited and waited but the truck didn't budge. Jimmy honked his horn with no result. Now about fifteen cars were backed up behind them and they too began honking their horns, frustrated at the inexplicably stalled traffic. It was just a stop sign. What was the hold-up?

Jimmy nudged Johnny. "Go and see what's goin' on."

Jumping out of the car and walking up to the cab of the truck, Johnny peered in and saw that there was no one inside. No driver, no passenger. No one. He stepped up on the running board to get a closer look but the result was the same. No one was in the truck.

The cars stopped along Sterling Place continued to honk their horns. It's a long street and the traffic was now backed up almost to Prospect Park.

Johnny walked back to the car and climbed back in the passenger seat.

He told Jimmy, "The truck, it's stuck there."

"What do you mean it's stuck there?"

Johnny sat staring out the front windshield of the car. He could barely hear his friend talking to him now. All of a sudden, he began to see it. It started coming back to him. Something that his mind refused to see when he had gone up to look at the truck. He saw it like a movie, playing in slow motion in his head. He's back at the front of the truck. He sees there is no one in it, but he sees something else. Something his mind cannot comprehend. Something so strange and out of place—so incomprehensible, so horrific-- it did not initially register in his brain. It was the entire tail section of a United Airlines jet. And it was leaning on the cab and the roof of the truck.

"What do you mean it's stuck there?!" Jimmy asked again.

"There's a friggin' plane in the street!"

It was the golden age of commercial airline flight. Nineteen fifty-nine was the first full year for the commercial jet, ushering in the "Jet Set" culture. Flying became fashionable and airlines were emphasizing the appealing fact that one could have lunch in Los Angeles and be back to New York in time for dinner. People dressed up to fly; women wore dresses and heels; men wore suits and ties. Seats were comfortable and roomy and the food and alcohol sumptuous and free. Of course, a person might spend five per cent of their annual salary on an airline flight. People living in Brooklyn, like Johnny Marrota, never even dreamed they would ever ride on an airplane. That was for rich people.

Not only did people pay five times the price for a plane ticket in the 1950s as we do today, passengers also had a five times greater chance of being killed.

These days, when you board a plane, you have a very good chance of landing safely on the other side. However, this was not the case in the early years. In 1959, for every 10 billion passenger miles flown, there were 72 fatalities. This may not seem like a high number, but compared to the years 2000-2010, when the number was 0.2 fatalities per 10 billion passenger miles it is clear that we have come very far in the area of aviation safety in the past 60 years. Less sophisticated flying technology was mostly to blame. "It wasn't safe to land in fog, so there were many crashes. Mid-air collisions were common," explained Guillaume de Syon, a professor at Pennsylvania's Albright College and an expert on aviation history. "Engines dropped out of planes so often that they weren't even recorded as accidents if the other engine could land them safely."[1] At the time, most larger airliners had four engines, and the reliability of one particular engine was so bad that several airliners were referred to by those who piloted them as "the best three engine airliners in the world."

In 1956, a United Airlines DC-7 and a TWA Super-Constellation, in relatively clear weather conditions and in broad daylight, collided over the wide-open spaces above the Grand Canyon killing all 128 passengers and crew on both planes. Up to that time, it was the worst aviation disaster in American history. The Eisenhower administration was aware of the problems plaguing the airways. Congressmen pursuing answers as to how this disaster could have occurred were shocked to discover how primitive the U.S. Air Traffic Control system was.

Adding to the risk, prior to the 1970's, the pilot was considered to be "God" in the cockpit and no one on the crew could or would question his actions or decisions. This attitude and culture, unfortunately, greatly increased the chance of accidents since human error can never be eliminated but input from others on the crew into the pilot's decisions has proven to go a long way to reducing human error accidents.

It would take many years, and many more accidents and fatalities and significant changes in technology, the air traffic control system, and the culture of the airline industry, before commercial aviation could brag of the safety record that exists today.

It was December 16, 1960. A young Senator from Massachusetts by the name of John Fitzgerald Kennedy had just been elected president, beating Vice President Richard Nixon in a closely contested election marking the end of the two-term presidency of Dwight D. Eisenhower.

Earlier that year, in February, four black college students in Greensboro, North Carolina, staged a sit-in at a segregated Woolworth lunch counter, protesting their denial of service, thus setting off a national campaign of sit-ins over the next eight months in support of Civil Rights.

In May, the Soviet Union shot down an American U-2 reconnaissance plane over Soviet airspace, capturing the pilot, Gary Powers.

In November, five paratroop battalions encircled the Presidential Palace in Saigon in what would be a failed coup attempt against the U.S. supported South Vietnamese President Nguyen Diem.

The first Teflon non-stick cookware went on sale at Macy's in New York.

NBC cancelled Howdy Doody after a 13-year run, the last episode airing September 24.

It was only weeks before Christmas. New York City stores were packed with shoppers all searching for that perfect gift or that great bargain. A woman shopping for a new suit for her son at Brooks Brothers Clothing could get one for $47.50. A man shopping for his wife at B. Altman & Co could pick up a quarter ounce bottle of Miss Dior cologne by Christian Dior for $12.50. The more frugal and practical housewife could get her husband some new BVD dress shirts of Belfast cotton for only $3.99 each.

Bonwit Teller's New York store announced they would be open Saturday, December 17, until 7:00 p.m. and every day the following week from 10:00 a.m. until 8:00 p.m.

Major stores were announcing new extended hours because of the snowstorm earlier in the week. Other merchants offered "reduced prices" because of the blizzard.

On Sunday afternoon, December 11 a rare pre-winter blizzard— the worst in thirteen years, and the heaviest early season snowfall in Weather Bureau records-- began its sweep through the New York metropolitan area, paralyzing transportation, closing schools and keeping hundreds of thousands from work. By 10 a.m. the next day, the temperature was 16 degrees, with wind gusts up to 35 miles an hour. Equally rare lightning and thunder flashed and echoed among the skyscrapers prompting many New Yorkers to call police to ask about explosions. A ten-minute display of lightning brightened the whole sky over Manhattan, accompanied by thunder that was muffled by the snow and the heavy overcast.

Commuter train and bus facilities struggled to keep operating around New York City. Of the city's 11,774 licensed cabs, fewer than 300 were in service during the morning hours. LaGuardia and Idlewild Airports in New York City and Newark and Teterboro in New Jersey shut down. Some commuters walked for miles from their Jersey homes to the mouth of the Lincoln Tunnel. Finding no buses there, they continued on foot through the 8,216 foot tube, arriving in New York exhausted and hours late for their jobs. All day, two lanes of the tunnel were closed to vehicular traffic so that the hardy pedestrians could walk to the city.

All schools were closed on the Monday of the storm with a late opening of 10 a.m. on Tuesday. Still, many children could not get to school if they relied on buses for transportation.

In the city seventeen persons died of heart attacks, many from over-exertion while shoveling snow or wading through drifts.

Hospitals complained that their driveways were blocked by stalled cars so that ambulances could not respond to emergency calls. Police radio cars took ambulance workers to calls until Sanitation Department tow trucks removed abandoned vehicles from driveways of Bellevue Hospital, Kings County Hospital, and Cumberland Hospital in Brooklyn.

The Department of Sanitation put an emergency force of 7,000 men to work cleaning the streets but traffic moved slowly and many side streets even in midtown were completely blocked by stalled automobiles. Abandoned and stalled cars littered the roads. Typical of Manhattan's traffic problem was on 50th Street in Rockefeller Center, where a combination of stalled cars and buses completely blocked East-West traffic.

The storm had dumped up to 17 inches of snow at the Battery and 20 inches in other parts of the city by the time is tapered off to flurries Monday afternoon, December 12. Schools reopened on the 13th with late arrival times and for some, no transportation.

By Wednesday, December 14, the city put 10,000 men and 3,000 pieces of heavy snow removal equipment into the job of clearing 6,045 miles of streets. The Sanitation Department, cancelling all days off, put 7,000 of its men on the job, plus 1,000 men from the five Borough Presidents' offices, and 2,000 others including temporary chauffeurs on the city payroll, operators of hired equipment and crews of private contractors. In addition, 800 privately owned trucks with drivers were hired at $8.48 to $15.75 an hour depending on the number of cubic yards of snow each could move.

The high temperature that day was 27, but the forecast was for temperatures warming into the 40 degree mark, which would serve to turn the remaining snow into a slushy mess.

By Wednesday, Dec 14, commuter train and bus service was nearly back on schedule and city schools were re-opened on a 10-to-4 schedule.

Things were getting back to normal and resilient New Yorkers got back to work, school, travel, Christmas shopping, and every other aspect of their everyday lives.

In Wilmette, Illinois, a quiet Chicago Suburb, 11-year-old Stephen Baltz lay fast asleep in his bed early Friday morning, Dec 16. The four-bedroom house sat on a tree lined street, surrounded by giant maples, oaks, and elms that provided a great place for a tire swing and kept the house shaded and cool in the hot Illinois summers. Above him was a ceiling painted sky blue from which were hung about a dozen World War I and World War II model planes he had built and painted. Suspended by wires, they appeared to be flying in the air over his bed. His white hamster, Snowball, silently trod the big wheel in his cage like a furry insomniac. Stevie and his friend Tom had long since given up their joint business venture to raise hamsters and sell them to the neighborhood kids. The hamsters bred all right, but the idea had fallen flat on the money-making end. Stevie would have attended Tom's brother's 12th birthday party that Friday, but for his trip to New York. On the wood-paneled walls of his room were pennants from all the Big 10 schools and a large poster of the solar system. With his keen curiosity, Stevie was well suited to pursue a career as a scientist, but what he really wanted to be was an FBI agent....or a corporate lawyer...or maybe an engineer for the Canadian Continental Railway. There would be plenty of time to decide that.

Stevie slept fitfully throughout the night. He was too excited to sleep well. He was about to travel on an airplane---and a jet at that!—all by himself. His mother had left for New York on Wednesday with his little sister Randee to visit their grandmother. Stevie was supposed to go with them, but he had a sore throat and was running a fever. The Baltz's didn't want to take a chance on

Stevie going on such a trip with an illness either present or pending, so his father got him a reservation for Friday, when he was finally in the clear to make the trip. Although Stevie would have liked to go with his mother, and sister, there was something very exciting about having the opportunity to fly on his own, so he wasn't all that disappointed when his parents told him he wouldn't be leaving on Wednesday with the others. Now the day was here!

He hopped out of bed at 5:45 a.m. and ran to his parents' room where his father, William Baltz, Sr. was sleeping soundly. Stevie excitedly shook his father awake. "Dad, come on, get up. I don't want to miss the plane!"

Baltz wanted to roll over and go back to sleep but he knew how excited his son was and how he was looking forward to the trip. Though the flight departure wasn't until 9:00 am, and O'Hare was a short 30 minutes' drive, there could be rush hour traffic to contend with. At least there was no snow expected today—at least not until that night.

The family maid, Pearl LeBlue, who the children called "Lady Blue" served Stephen and his father breakfast but Stevie couldn't eat much. He just sat there dressed in his best gray suit and grinned. The house seemed empty without his mother and his little sister. Randee could be a nuisance now and then, but Stephen had to admit to himself that the house was lonely with just "the men" and he missed them. He would see them soon. He was ready to be off on his big adventure.

Grabbing Stevie's small suitcase, William Baltz gulped down the rest of his coffee and motioned to his son that it was time to go. The car was warm and snug in the garage, so it wouldn't take long to warm it up. That was a good thing. The temperature was just under 20 degrees and if the car had been out all night, it would take a lot of warming up to get it going.

Smiling contentedly to each other, father and son took off for O'Hare.

Captain Robert Sawyer left his home in Hemet, California for the Los Angeles airport around 3pm Thursday, December 15th. He lived 70 miles from the airport—a good two hour drive-- and since he was scheduled to fly out after midnight, he slept in the company's airport quarters from 5pm until 11.[2] First Officer Robert Fiebing, and Second Officer Richard Prewitt met Sawyer at the airport and together they boarded their empty United Air Lines DC-8 in Los Angeles at 12:20 a.m. Friday morning and headed for Chicago. They would pick up their four-member cabin crew and all their passengers there, and with the flight number of United 826, they would depart for New York at 8:11 a.m. CST. The United Airlines Douglas DC-8 was part of the new breed of passenger carrier, just completing its first year of commercial service. Its four turbojet engines allowed it to cruise at 550 miles per hour. Commercial pilots loved the power and speed of the new jets over the conventional turboprop planes they were used to flying up until about a year ago.

Robert Sawyer, at 46, was a twenty-year veteran of United Airlines, having joined the airline in January of 1941. It was his first love since he was a boy and there was never anything more thrilling to him than flying. When he was a teenager, he and a friend rebuilt an old World War I Waco bi-plane and flew it after only a few hours' instruction. Sawyer had flown with United under the Air Transport Command during WWII and flew many different aircraft types since signing on with United, but the DC-8 was his first jet and he was qualified to fly it in June. The speed of the new jets entering the commercial fleets appealed to Sawyer, who also enjoyed racing cars.

Born in Wayne, PA, raised in Rochester, NY, Sawyer moved to California at 19 to attend college. After the war, with his wife, Pat, he set up a 20-acre ranch at 1001 Penfield Road in Hemet CA., where he had room to raise horses and cattle, something he loved almost as much as flying. At the age of 11, he had won a New York state riding championship. As a teenager he was declared reserve champion at the Madison Square Garden Horse Show. He was proud and thrilled that his three daughters, Pam, 14, Robin, 13, and Kim, 8 shared his enthusiasm and talents. Just the past June, Pam rode her horse Hi Hopes in the 15th annual National Horse Show at Del Mar, California.

Robert Fiebing, Sawyer's first officer, shared the captain's love of horses. Just before today's flight, he had been working on a stable at the family home, 23126 Dolorosa St, in Woodland Hills, CA. All the kids in the neighborhood were giving Bob Fiebing a hand in the building. The Fiebings—Bob, his wife Lorraine, and two sons, David, 8, and Danny 6, were getting a horse for Christmas. Bob had bought the family Christmas tree before he left and it was there leaning against the porch of their redwood ranch house. When he returned from New York, the family would bring the tree inside and spend a lovely family evening decorating it.

The flight engineer, Richard Eugene (Gene) Prewitt, 30 years old, had been with United for five years. He was qualified on the DC-8 one year ago. Prewitt grew up in Texas, but moved to Torrance California with his wife, Millie eight years ago. In California, they had their four children: Susan, 8; Judy, 6; Cynthia, 4; and Richard, 2. Tomorrow, the family was planning to celebrate the birthdays of Judy, Cindy, and little Ricky at their home at 256 W. 226th Place. Though the 17th of December was only Ricky's birthday, Cindy had turned four November 29th, and Judy had turned six last Tuesday. Prewitt looked forward to the party and trimming the family Christmas tree. but he couldn't shake a dream he had Wednesday night. When he woke on Thursday morning, he began to tell Millie about it: "I had a dream about a plane crash. It was so real I can still remember the number on the plane." But Millie stopped him. "Don't tell me it! I'm superstitious." So, he told her no more about it.

Putting the thoughts of families, parties, and ominous dreams behind them, the three men climbed into the cockpit of their DC-8, registration number N8013U and headed for Chicago.

5

They came from all parts of the country: Colorado, Idaho, California, Washington, Nevada, Iowa. They all had somewhere to go. Flying back home after a business trip. Flying to a business meeting. Flying home for the holidays. Flying to New York for a shopping trip or a long-awaited and planned adventure.

Several passengers arose early in the west to get on planes to meet United's 8:00 a.m. connecting flight out of Chicago for New York. Lowell Bowen, Edna Parker, and Beverly Parks left from San Francisco. Beverly had a long trip ahead of her—she was on her way to Nova Scotia to visit her mother. She had just quit her job with Pacific Southwest Airlines where she was a flight attendant. Recently engaged, she was looking forward to sharing the exciting news with her family.

Two passengers left from Seattle: Donald Freese, a United Airlines agent was heading out for a vacation trip to New York and Earl Reams, Chief Mate of the steamship Steel Recorder, looked forward to spending the holidays back east with his family in New York. Earl Riley left his Washington state home for the early flight to get back to Rhode Island for his father's funeral. It was a sad day, as this was the second death in the family just since Thanksgiving, and though Earl was not looking forward to the trip, he soldiered on.

Thursday night, in Boise, Idaho, the entire Boise Basque community gathered for a farewell party for 27-year-old Ricardo Garamendi. The Basque sheepherder was returning to his native Spain after completing his three-year sheepherding contract in the Mountain Home, Idaho area. The party moved to the airport just as the plane was about to take off. But Garamendi didn't rush to get on just yet. He wanted to purchase flight insurance and couldn't decide how much to take out. His friends tried to hurry him along. "You're going to miss your flight if you don't make up your mind!" they prodded him. Garamendi finally decided on $150,000. At the current exchange rate, that would amount to over ten and a half million pesetas for the beneficiary—his mother--a huge fortune in Spain. He laid down five one-dollar bills for the full coverage policy. Then he wanted a receipt, saying, "I might need it in case I lose an arm or a leg!" The small group hurried outside to where the plane waited, just readying for take-off. The ramp had already been removed, and the plane had started taxiing out. Ricardo's friends flagged it down and when the crew saw the little party rushing out to the plane, they stopped, rolled the ramp back up, opened up the door, and Ricardo boarded. His friends stood and waved a fond farewell as they watched the plane take off.

In Wisconsin, 18-year-old Susan Gordon, a freshman at the University of Wisconsin signed out of campus on Friday morning. She was going home to New York to spend holidays with her family, and she was excited. "Suzy Gordon", she wrote in the log, "— destination: New York---Home!! Woopee!" She wrote in the "date return column" Jan 2, 5:30 pm.

In Omaha, Nebraska, another college student was rising early to make his way east. Darnell Mallory, had been away from home for almost four months and was anxious to return to Summit, NJ and spend the holidays with his family. The 19-year-old had just earned his first collegiate football letter at Omaha University as a freshman. He had suffered a hip injury in Omaha's opening game and hadn't reached his anticipated potential, but Coach Al Caniglia felt that Mallory would be a great asset to the team in his final three years. Earlier that week, his friend and fellow Summit native Barry Miller approached Mallory and asked him to share expenses on a Christmas holiday trip home that weekend. Mallory declined because he didn't have any Friday classes so had purchased a ticket on United to fly home Friday morning. He was making rapid progress with the University basketball team after reporting late and appeared capable of becoming a January starter. Mallory had gotten permission to skip the junior varsity basketball game with Nebraska Wesleyan University Friday night so he could make his Friday morning flight.

It was early morning in Des Moines, Iowa when 21-year-old Ardythe Lee woke her mother. She was booked on a 6:15 a.m. flight to Chicago where she'd make a connection to New York. She had time off for a four-day holiday to visit a Des Moines girlfriend, Sue Decker, who was now living in New York. Sue's mother, had given Ardythe the family's Christmas gifts for her daughter. Ardythe's father worked nights for the Des Moines Register and Tribune newspaper. He bid his daughter good-bye as he trundled off to bed, just as she and her mother were leaving for the airport. His daughter had flown before in smaller planes but this was to be her first trip in a jet. And she was excited about her first trip to New York.

Iowa State University sophomore James Mountain boarded a plane Friday morning for Chicago. He was flying to New York to visit his family for the holidays. This Christmas would be special, as he would be introducing his parents to his new fiancée, Sharon Packard, who was also a student at Iowa State. Sharon had class on Friday, so wouldn't be flying with Jim. Best he go ahead anyway, and prepare his parents for the news. She would follow him the next day.

Patricia Spear and Becky Woodward drove around Tuesday night, Dec 13, talking about things most young college-aged women talk about. They were close friends in Salt Lake City and Becky had enrolled as a freshman at University of Utah last fall after her family moved to Dobbs Ferry, NY. Patricia was driving, and jokingly remarked to Becky, "I remember my father once telling me that, the way I drive I was going to get into an accident." Becky replied, "'Well, I ride in quite a few planes and I think that if I ever get killed it will be in a plane." Becky was flying home to New York to visit her family for the Christmas holidays and leaving Friday. So was Frank DiLeo, a 21-year-old physical education junior at Utah from Floral Park, Long Island. Becky used to date Frank's roommate Jack and, at a party, she and Frank discovered with delight that they had reservations aboard the same New York bound plane. When they left early Friday morning, Frank's roommate, Jack, was at the airport to see them both off. [3]

Albert Bock had recently won a promotion to superintendent of Midwestern operations of Wyman-Gorman Co., makers of airplane landing gear and wing struts for the government. The new position required him to fly from his home near Boston, Massachusetts to Chicago on business at least once a week. He thought no more of flying than most people would about taking a train or a car. Normally Bock would return home on Friday night, giving him most of the day Friday in Chicago to finish up work there. But his wife had had a birthday on Wednesday and Bock had missed it so he scheduled himself on an early flight out of Chicago on Friday morning so he could get home and surprise her with a party that evening to belatedly celebrate with friends.

Dorothy Miner had planned a flight out of Chicago on the past Sunday. Her stepmother was to undergo surgery and Dorothy, a registered nurse, told her father she would take time off from her job at the University of Illinois Hospital to fly home to Ramsey, NJ and help out. But when Sunday came, a blizzard was slamming New York and the entire eastern seaboard and her flight was cancelled. Dorothy changed her reservations for Tuesday. The storm was expected to have cleared by then, but then Dayton, Ohio was hit with a city-wide power failure, causing yet again more flight cancellations, including her flight to New York. "Third time's the charm," she must have thought to herself as she yet again rescheduled her flight back east for Friday, December 16.

Twenty-two-year-old Carlos Jose Wittmer was on his way home to Caracas, Venezuela. He and his young wife, Olga had been living in Chicago for a year while Carlos attended Industrial Engineering College. He spent eleven months at the college along with his cousin, Juan. Both took extra classes nights and Saturdays to speed their training. Carlos received his diploma from the school Thursday, and originally had planned to leave Chicago Sunday. But he was anxious to get home. The couple had a new addition to the family—a son, Carlos, Jr. born November 7th and they were eager for the child to meet his grandparents. Anxious to go home after a year's absence, the young couple decided on an earlier flight. Minor problems plagued the Wittmers their last few days in Chicago. Carlos' diploma needed endless certifications by city, county, and embassy officials; a newly designed ring wasn't ready, but Carlos took the sample anyway and proudly wore it when he departed on Friday. Back home, Carlos had a job waiting with Industry Electrical Venezuela in Caracas.

Catherine Post, 18-year-old Freshman at Medill School of Journalism at Northwestern University in Evanston, Illinois, arrived early at O'Hare airport in Chicago, escorted by her friend John Riley, who was a fellow student at Medill. She was hoping to get on a flight to New York and get home to see her family for the holidays, but she didn't have a ticket. At the ticket counter, she got lucky. Another college freshman, 18-year-old Leslie Picker, had cancelled her reservation on United at the last minute in favor of a non-stop flight from California, where she attended college at Berkeley, to New York where her family lived. Catherine was given Leslie's spot on the plane.

Booked on United Flight 826 from Chicago to New York on December 16 was Edmund Hillary, conqueror of Mount Everest.

Hillary had booked space on the Friday flight for himself, a Sherpa guide, Khumjo Chumbi, and Desmond Doig, an English writer, but his schedule in Chicago that Friday prevented him from being able to leave just then. Hillary transferred the reservation to a Saturday flight.

When Capt. Robert Sawyer landed his United DC-8 plane in Chicago after their flight from Los Angeles, four flight attendants joined him, first officer Fiebing, and flight engineer Prewitt for the short follow-up flight to New York. Ann Marie Bouthan hadn't seen her large family of 14 brothers and sisters in eighteen months. She worked out of Los Angeles and they lived in New York. They were all looking forward to the holiday season visit from their globe-trotting sibling. Augustine Ferrar was fresh off a holiday shopping trip with her roommate Mary Lee Ostendorf in Manhattan Beach, California. Ferrar was hurrying to buy her Christmas gifts. She hadn't been scheduled to fly until Saturday but traded her shift three times with other stewardesses to be sure she could get back east a day early. Twenty-three-year-old Patricia Keller, a flight attendant for only six months, and twenty-four-year-old Mary Mahoney, a flight attendant for United for three years, rounded out the United crew.

Meanwhile, in Dayton, Ohio, five crew members and fifteen passengers waited in the early morning hours to board TWA flight 266 to New York, with a stopover in Columbus. There were seven flights that left Dayton for New York daily, and normally, there would be 35 or 40 persons aboard this flight, but today, there was only the fifteen.

TWA First Officer Dean Bowen was usually off on Fridays but was substituting on the Dayton to New York route because last week's storm in the east has forced changes in the work schedule

TWA flight engineer, 30-year-old Leroy Rosenthal had just married seven weeks ago. He and his new bride now lived in Long Island while Leroy flew out of New York for TWA. He loved to fly, especially with the chance it gave him to see the world. He has just returned from an eight-day flight to Portugal, Spain, Germany, France, Italy, Greece, and Egypt.

Flight attendants Margaret Gernat and Patricia Post boarded the TWA Constellation for the short flight to New York. Margaret, who had been a flight attendant for two years, would be turning 25 in two days and was looking forward to spending her birthday and Christmas with her family in Granville, NY. Twenty-one-year-old Patty Ann Post had only been a flight attendant less than year, but she always loved to fly so it was a natural career choice for her. She joined TWA in January and received her Air Hostess wings that April. In February, Patty sat down and wrote a thoughtful letter to her family. She was writing the letter, she said, "just in case I am ever involved in one of those 'one in a million' air accidents," and added: *"Truthfully, I have a great deal of confidence in flying, otherwise I wouldn't be in this job...To me, it's like a dream I had as a little girl that have finally come true."*

She continued: *"Now that I'm away from home, I've found out how much you all really mean to me. I guess I didn't realize at the time but now when I look back, I must have been pretty miserable to live with at times. All that groping around, and sulking, and feeling sorry for myself. I really am ashamed for the way I treated everyone. After all that you have done for me and have given me, I can't understand why I wasn't more appreciative. I guess I was too self-centered and immature to realize the way I was acting. I hope I've grown up a little since then. I'd never, in a million years, be able*

to thank you for everything you've given me. .... Daddy, mother,
Bobbie and Jon, I hope you all have long, healthy, happy lives.
Daddy, don't you work too hard. I'm so grateful that we finally got
to really know each other. Mother, thanks for standing by me during
all my 'little' problems and for being the best mother anyone could
ever wish for.... I'm surely glad I had you all as my family, I'm
awfully lucky! Please take good care of yourselves and thank you
again for everything. I love you all so much. God bless you." The
letter was signed, *"all my love, Patti."* It was never mailed. [4]

TWA lead ticket agent, Ken Ringlespaugh talked to the two
hostesses before the plane left Dayton. They wanted to know if
they would be busy—they normally served breakfast after the plane
left Columbus. They were happy to learn that the number of
passengers would not be too heavy.

Sixty-year old Carter Helton, was en route to Boston to the
bedside of his 19-year-old son Michael a student at Babson
Institute, who was being treated for tuberculosis at a Boston
hospital. Doctors said he was well enough along in his recovery to
make the trip home to Dayton to be with his family at Christmas
before he'd have to return for six more weeks of treatment.
Carter's wife, Harriett, was already in Boston.

TWA ticket counter agent, Salvadore Lepe greeted Edward
Tierney, a 34-year old textile engineer for the Dayton Rubber
Company. Tierney was in a jovial mood and remarked to Lepe
about his quick trip east. He'd be turning around and coming right
back on Saturday. [5]

Murray T. Wright, of North Ferrisburg, Vermont, a specialist in
General Electric missile development, was returning from Wright-
Patterson Air Force Base in Dayton to the Burlington, Vermont
plant. His coworker, George Keenan, an engineer in GE's
engineering department in Schenectady, was returning from

Chicago to New York that same day. Keenan was aboard United 826.

Warren Petersen, staff engineer for the Republic Aircraft Company, Arthur Swenson, project engineer of the Pratt-Whitney Aircraft Corp, and John Walden, salesman for West Virginia Pulp and Paper Co. rounded out the fifteen Dayton boarding passengers whose final destination was New York. Walden's bag was lost when he arrived in Dayton but the airline found it for him. He called TWA the next day and spoke to the lead ticket agent, Ken Ringlespaugh. "I think you owe me something', he said. Walden was on the waiting lists for all the return flights to New York. Ringlespaugh told him that he could take the 7:40 am flight—TWA 266—there was no waiting list. "You'd think I'd given him the moon, he was quite gratified—he shouldn't have been. He even stopped at the counter to thank me for getting him the seat before the plane took off—but I was busy in the back and didn't see him." [6]

Juanita Mullins dashed through the terminal doorway at the Dayton airport and almost ran smack into the TWA ticket counter where agent Salvadore Lepe stood. He had just seen all the passengers boarded onto TWA Flight 266. At least he *thought* he had everyone. "My husband is parking the car—we couldn't get a spot! Has the plane left yet?" Juanita asked. In her arms, she clutched her three-month-old daughter, Tracy Lynn, wrapped snuggly in a pink blanket. Lepe thought it was the prettiest little baby he had ever seen. Then Lepe saw Cecil Mullins fly through the doorway. There was no time to talk—Lepe hurried to get them onto the plane which was just about to take off. The Mullins were on their way to Puerto Rico to Juanita's parents who had yet to see their little granddaughter. But first, they would be making a stop in New York to visit two of Juanita's old friends and nursing school roommates. [7] Juanita, whose husband called her "Winnie" had wanted to make her trip a surprise. Her cousin, Amauris Cabudis had asked her 'when you come?'" In her heavily accented English, the young nurse replied coyly, 'I not tell you.'"[8]

Six other passengers boarded whose final destination was Columbus.

One reservation went unfilled on the TWA flight from Dayton: that of 21-year-old Winslow Dill, a Wilberforce University student from Bermuda. Dill was flying via New York to Bermuda to visit his ailing mother but was unable to get to the bank on time on Thursday to withdraw the money he would need for the ticket. He solicited his friends for a loan but was unable to raise enough to buy his ticket.

TWA 266 left Dayton at 7:40 a.m.

In Columbus, First Officer Dean Bowen was readying for the 9:00 follow-on flight to New York when he ran into an old friend he hadn't seen in nearly four years. "Hi Dean, old boy, how are you," said James Porter. Porter, who was at the Columbus airport preparing to board another TWA Constellation of which he was the co-pilot, had not seen Bowen in about four years. The two young men were roommates in Kansas City in 1953 and Bowen later served as an usher at Porter's wedding. There was only time for a brief greeting and Bowen did not have time to introduce Porter to TWA Captain David Wollam, who was to be piloting their Constellation that morning. [9] Thirty-nine-year-old Wollam, had been an Air Force flight instructor during WWII and worked for TWA for the past 15 years. He grew up and lived in California until 1954 when he moved with his wife and two small children to Huntington, NY.

After changing to a new aircraft in Columbus, Captains Wollam and Bowen and their compliment of flight attendants boarded 30 more passengers for the continuing flight to New York. Six of the fifteen passenger who boarded in Dayton disembarked in Columbus. Nine continued the flight to New York.

Nancy Briggs, 19-year-old Ohio State University Junior arrived at the airport in Columbus, Ohio on her way home to Springfield,

Massachusetts to spend the holidays with her family. She reluctantly bid farewell to her new fiancée and fellow OSU student Lenny Hart. "I'm afraid I'll never see you again," Nancy ominously told him before boarding the TWA Constellation for New York.[10]

Vincent Flood sat in the boarding area for TWA Flight 266 to New York. As he stared down at the boarding pass in his hand he felt it stared back at him reproachfully. He was heading home, and he was happy about that, but he felt like a failure and wasn't sure how his family was going to accept it. Vincent had made the difficult decision to leave St. Joseph's Priory in Somerset, Ohio. He had only just begun his studies as a Dominican novice four months ago, and though he was a good student, it became quickly apparent to him that the priesthood was not the vocation for him. Now he would have to sit down and explain it all to his parents, and seven brothers and sisters—siblings which included a Jesuit priest and three nuns.

Peter Griebel, 24, and his wife Karen bundled their three-week-old daughter Jennifer against the cold morning air and headed out to Port Columbus Airport. It had been a big decision to leave his Columbus job with the Fuller Brush Company to look for new work and set up a new home in New Jersey. But first, the little family was going to Newton, Connecticut to visit Peter's stepfather and show off the new baby. Then the family would be taking up residence with Peter's grandparents in Weston, NJ. They had prepared the lower level section of their house on Norfield Road for occupancy by the Griebels. The grandparents had been looking forward to having Griebel and his family with them to celebrate their 47th wedding anniversary Christmas day.

Also on Thursday night, five young men, all Ohio State University students and fraternity brothers gathered to celebrate the graduation of their friend Tim Goebel who would be receiving his degree in business administration at commencement exercises on Friday. David Evans and Dick Magnuson were sorry they were going to miss the ceremony, but they had reservations on a flight to New York. On Friday morning, Evans and Magnuson were together with their fraternity brothers Tom Hartman, Tim Goebel, and Warren Hickmott, to see Evans and Magnuson off at the Columbus airport. They were heading back east to visit family, and Evans was going along to help Magnuson drive back with his new auto—a Christmas present from his parents.

The Trans World Airlines plane that Wollam and Bowen would be flying on the hour and half flight to LaGuardia was a Lockheed L-1049 Super Constellation, nicknamed a "Connie." The aircraft was Lockheed's response to Douglas's very successful DC-6 airliner which started flying in 1950. The Super Constellation had its first flight in July of 1951 with Eastern Airlines. TWA began flying the Connie in 1952. It sported a very distinctive triple tail, with red stripes across the fins. Bolted to each of its wings were two of the same propeller-driven engines that had powered B-29 bombers in the Korean War. The craft that was flying to New York today had joined the TWA fleet in 1952. By December 1960, TWA's original 1049 Super Constellations were being eclipsed by the jets in prestige and demand—they were no longer considered modern, and TWA had begun to phase them out. TWA operated ten 1049 Super Constellations of the same type—one had already been lost in the mid-air collision over the Grand Canyon in 1956.

6

A cold front had passed during the night and changed light rain and drizzle to snow in the central and northern portions of Ohio, so the TWA flight plan called for Instrument Flight Rules (IFR). The flight path was to LaGuardia Airport via Appleton, Ohio, Johnstown, Pennsylvania, Selmsgrove, Pennsylvania, and finally to LaGuardia Airport. The way points were VHF Omnidirectional Range (VOR) points—short range radio beacons which transmit signals to aircraft receivers to determine their position and keep them on course.

Captain Sawyer and his crew of United 826 departed Chicago O'Hare at 9:11 a.m. Eastern Standard Time. *[All times hereafter are Eastern Standard Time unless otherwise indicated]* They reached their cruising altitude of 27,000 feet at 9:36. The flight to the New York area was normal and routine. With little over one hour flying time ahead of them, the passengers undoubtedly settled themselves in with a magazine or a cup of coffee and conversation with their seat mate. Eleven-year old Stephen Baltz took his seat in the rear of the aircraft. His parents probably thought that would be the best place for him because it would put him in close proximity to the flight attendants in case he needed any help during the flight. Stephen stared out the window as the DC-8 took off. Watching the ground quickly recede below him and objects on it grow smaller and smaller, Stephen felt at the same time tiny and big; he was a big, grown-up boy, flying over the countryside all by himself.

United 826 and TWA 266 uneventfully travelled their designated routes, being handed off to different traffic control regions as they entered their sectors. When the planes got within 20 miles of the New York City airspace, the New York Route Traffic Control Center took over to give them guidance on landing, weather conditions, and instructions on entering holding patterns as other aircraft were systematically guided in to the two largest New York airports: Idlewild (now called John F. Kennedy International) and LaGuardia, both located in Queens.

Air Traffic Controller Ron DiGiovanni was at New York Center that morning working the radar, handling incoming traffic on a route called Airway Victor 30 that crossed New Jersey twenty miles north of Trenton. John Fisher and Harold Brown were working as a team with DiGiovanni. Fisher managed flight data on the planes entering the sector, writing the codes which indicated the aircraft's origin, destination, airline, flight number, aircraft type, altitude and estimated time to its next checkpoint on a strip of paper inserted into a metal holder. Brown worked the telephones communicating with tower controllers. DiGiovanni transferred airline and flight number information from the strips Fisher lined up to smaller paper strips that he inserted into plastic markers called "shrimp boats." DiGiovanni then lined up the shrimp boats on the side of the radar screen in the order in which he expected them to enter his sector. Once he identified the appropriate "target" he would place the identifying shrimp boat next to it. Shrimp boats were moved along the board tracking the progress of the flights under his direction. All the while, DiGiovanni, as the radarman, had to keep in his head the altitude, speed, and heading of the aircraft, giving them new directions (vectors) when needed, and preserving their separation in airspace. [11]

At 10:19 the TWA piston engine prop Constellation--Flight 266--reported in to the New York Center. The plane was passing Allentown, PA at 11,000 feet, and the New York Center cleared the flight to the Linden intersection and cleared it to descend to 10,000.

About this same time, Captain Sawyer and First Officer Fiebing in United 826 noticed that one of their navigation receivers was inoperative. While this did not prevent the pilots from being able to navigate—there was a second receiver they could use—it did hamper them. The pilots would now have to continuously switch radio frequencies between two VOR stations. More attention would have to be paid, and more complicated calculations would have to be made, to compensate for the loss of the second receiver--and it had to be done quickly, at the speed the plane was travelling. Pilots were trained to handle this, so Sawyer and Fiebing, though reporting the problem to Aeronautical Radio, Incorporated-- operator of United Air Lines' aeronautical communications system --they did not inform New York Center of their loss of the navigational receiver.

At about 10:21, Ron DiGiovanni in the New York Center took over control of the United flight which was heading east along Victor 30. Picking up the target on his radar, DiGiovanni confirmed that it was United 826, and marked the blip with a shrimp boat. DiGiovanni called Flight 826: *"United 826 New York Center, radar contact,"* and issued the pilot clearance to descend to 13,000 feet. United 826 replied, *"Roger, we're cleared to 13,000...If we're going to have a delay we would rather hold upstairs than down. We're going to need three quarters of a mile; do you have the weather handy?"* The Center replied, *"No, but I'll get it, there have been no delays until now."* The weather report provided to Sawyer a few minutes later of 1500 foot overcast with a half mile visibility in light snow confirmed for him that the skies over New York were murky and Sawyer thought it preferable, if he had to go into a holding pattern, he would rather stay as long as possible at a higher altitude where the atmosphere was clearer before descending and entering into the pattern at a lower altitude.

After reporting that they were "starting down," at approximately 10:25, DiGiovanni amended the clearance given to the United pilot. *"826 cleared to proceed on Victor 30 until intercepting Victor 123 and that way to Preston. It'll be a little bit quicker."* The new routing shortened the distance to the Preston intersection by approximately 11 miles. With their one malfunctioning radio receiver, this shortening of their approach to the airport would require rapid mental recalculations and interpretation of a display that could easily be misread.

At 10:27, TWA 266 informed New York Center that they were past the Solberg, New Jersey VOR. Since the plane was nearing its final descent for LaGuardia, New York Center terminated radio service with instructions to contact LaGuardia Control. At LaGuardia, Air Traffic Controller William Smith took the hand off. Smith radioed the TWA pilot, Captain David Wollam, to confirm his position and instructed the TWA to slow its approach speed and descend to 5,000 feet as it followed Victor 6, which would put him on course to cross Staten Island five miles south of Newark Airport.

At approximately 10:30, New York Center also cleared United 826 to descend to 5,000 feet. The jet reported leaving 14,000 feet. *"Roger, looks like you'll be able to make Preston at five,"* the Center told Sawyer, who replied *"Er, will head it right on down, we'll dump it."* (aviation slang for coming down in a hurry.) DiGiovanni warned Sawyer that he might be held up at Preston and "stacked" in an elliptical pattern until Idlewild was ready for him to land. He gave the pilots the holding pattern instructions.

Once United 826 confirmed the instructions to hold at Preston until receiving further direction from Idlewild, DiGiovanni signed off, telling Captain Sawyer to contact Idlewild approach controllers to direct him from there. *"826, Roger, and you received the holding instructions at Preston, radar service is terminated. Contact Idlewild Approach Control one two three point seven. Good day."* Flight 826 acknowledged "Good day" at approximately 10:33. Then DiGiovanni turned to address three other flights in his sector. Captain Sawyer switched frequencies and radioed Idlewild approach controller Herbert Rausch that he was headed to the Preston holding area, transmitting: *"Idlewild Approach Control,*

United 826, approaching Preston at 5,000." It was 10:33 a.m. This was the last transmission from the flight. The DC-8 was not "approaching Preston." It had shot past it at over 300 miles an hour.

Just a minute before, LaGuardia had cleared TWA 266 to continue its descent to 5,000 feet. Controller William Smith suddenly observed an unidentified target on the edge of his radar scope. The target was moving in from the southwest in a northeasterly direction and was then about six miles below the TWA plane on his scope. Smith advised Captain Wollam in the Constellation, *"traffic at 2:30, six miles northeast-bound."* He then asked Wollam for his altitude. The reply was garbled and Smith asked if he heard "5,500" correctly. TWA 266 replied in the affirmative. Smith issued Wollam clearance to continue his descent to 1,500 feet.

About a minute later, Smith once again advised Wollam of the unidentified traffic in his area: *"Roger, that appears to be jet traffic off your right now at 3 o'clock at one mile, northeast-bound."* Suddenly, the two targets merged into one on Smith's radar screen. This wasn't at first as alarming as it may seem. Since radar at that time could not detect the altitude of the planes being tracked, blips converging on a radar screen may have created the appearance of a collision, but in reality, the planes could be separated by at least one thousand feet in altitude. The controller had no way of knowing without a direct report from the pilot as to their altitude. As the radar completed another sweep, Smith suddenly became alarmed. His target—TWA 266 hadn't moved at all. At 10:33, a noise similar to that caused by an open microphone was heard for six seconds duration from TWA 266. Then there was silence.

At Idlewild, Herbert Rausch, not realizing he had already lost United 826, continued to communicate with the aircraft providing instructions. *"United 826, this is Idlewild Approach Control,* maintain 5,000. Little or no delay at Preston. Idlewild landing runway four right, ILS in use. Idlewild weather- 600 scattered, estimated 1,500 overcast; visibility 1/2-mile, light rain and fog. Altimeter 29.63, over." The transmission was completed at approximately 10:33. It was never acknowledged. Subsequent attempts to contact United 826 were unsuccessful. Radio communications with other aircraft during this period were normal, so Rausch knew his radio was not malfunctioning. When Rausch looked on his radar screen a few seconds later, he could not find the United DC-8.

Controllers at Idlewild continued to try to raise United 826.

United Eight Twenty-six, Idlewild Approach Control.

United Eight Twenty-six, Idlewild Approach Control.

United Eight Twenty-six, this is Idlewild Approach Control.

United Eight Twenty-six, this is Idlewild Approach Control.

United Eight Twenty-six, this is Idlewild Approach Control.

United Eight Twenty-six, this is Idlewild Approach Control...uh...broadcasting in the blind. Reply transponder and ident.

United Eight Twenty-six, this is Idlewild Approach Control.

United Eight Twenty-six, this is Idlewild Approach Control, how do you hear?

United Jet Eight Twenty-six, United Jet Eight Twenty-six, this is Idlewild Approach Control. If you receive, answer one-two three point seven, one one nine point seven, one nineteen point one, one two one point one, or....uh, frequency one two three point nine.

United Jet Eight Twenty-six, United Jet Eight Twenty-six, this is Idlewild Approach Control. If you receive, reply code forty-five, reply code forty-five.

United Jet Eight Twenty-six, United Jet Eight Twenty-six, Idlewild radar, if you hear, reply code forty-five, reply code forty-five.

Meanwhile, at LaGuardia, William Smith continued to try to raise TWA 266.

And Trans World Two Sixty-Six, turn further left one zero zero.

Trans World Two Sixty-Six turn further left one zero zero

Trans World Two Sixty-Six, this is La Guardia… er… Approach Control, one, two, three, four, five, five, four, three, two, one. How do you read, Trans World Two Sixty-Six?

Trans World Two Sixty-Six, La Guardia Approach Control, one, two, three, four, five, five, four, three, two, one. If you read turn right heading three six zero.

Trans World Two Sixty-Six, La Guardia Approach Control, one, two, three, four, five, five, four, three, two, one, how do you read?

Trans World Two Sixty-Six, La Guardia Approach Control, time now one five three four zulu [Greenwich Mean Time, or 10:34 a.m. New York time] If you read, turn right heading three six zero. Turn right heading three six zero. Trans World Two Sixty-Six.

Trans World Two Sixty-Six, La Guardia Approach Control, the time is now one five three five zulu. If you read, turn right heading three six zero. Turn right heading three six zero. Trans World Two Sixty Six.

Trans World Two Sixty-Six, this is La Guardia Approach Control, one, two, three, four, five, four, three, two, one. If you read, come up on any frequency that you have, sir, any frequency that you have. If you read, also turn right three six zero.

Trans World Two Sixty-Six, this is La Guardia Approach Control. One, two, three, four, five, four, three, two, one. Trans World Two Sixty-Six, La Guardia Approach. If you read, turn right heading three six zero. Turn right heading three six zero. Hold that heading for one minute for radar identification, Trans World Two Sixty-Six.

Trans World Two Sixty-Six, this is La Guardia Approach, time is now one five three six. If you read turn right heading three six zero. Turn right heading three six zero, Trans World Two Sixty Six.

At 10:39, Idlewild controllers reaching another plane warned: *"We have a lost aircraft and we see a target directly over the radio beacon. We do not know his intentions."*

LaGuardia then radioed to the New York Center.

Hello New York. This is LaGuardia, I think we've got an emergency. Nobody declared anything. But who is that jet or fast-moving aircraft that went from Preston toward Flatbush?

From Preston toward Flatbush? New York Center queried.

LaGuardia controllers were now becoming frantic. *Yes. He's at Flatbush right now.*

Er, a fast-moving aircraft—going where? Do you know his destination?

I don't know—I think he may have-- now, listen-- to this. He may have hit one of our aircraft! We're not sure.

All right. Just stand by.

He's now a mile inside Flatbush.

All right. Stand by one.

New York, New York

Go ahead, La Guardia. What do you have?

All right, now we got troubles, but we're not sure of it. We lost contact with a TWA, Two Six Six, I believe his number is. He was on a collision course with an aircraft, an unknown aircraft heading northeast from Preston towards Flatbush. That aircraft now is a mile outside the LaGuardia outer marker, heading northeast-bound.

The unknown—you still have the unknown in radar contact?

No, we're not talking to the unknown, but we see him, yes.

All right. Okay.

Okay, see if you can find out anything about him. Let us know immediately.

Will do

LaGuardia Approach Control called the Airport tower and told them, *"I think we have trouble here with a TWA Connie---there's something wrong—he's not moving or anything. He might have got hit, uh, by another airplane."* The tower acknowledged but could offer no help or additional information. LaGuardia Approach Control then contacted Idlewild.

Idlewild. LaGuardia, Idlewild Approach, LaGuardia Approach Control

Uh, is that your traffic at... uh... Flatbush?

Just a minute. In the background, the controller could be heard asking someone: *"Is that your traffic at Flatbush?"*

No it's not our traffic, LaGuardia

Idlewild Approach was not aware of the shortcut given the United plane, nor the fact that the jet had failed to hold over Preston, and so was not expecting the jet for another ten minutes or so. They had never picked up and identified the DC-8 in their sector on radar.

Well now, he's--- we lost communications with an aircraft, and, ah, something may be wrong with him.

Just a minute

Our traffic that went up Flatbush there.

Wait a minute La Guardia. The controller asked others in the control room, *"Do you think that might be him? One over Flatbush?"* Then replied to LaGuardia, *"It could be ours on approach control, New York."*

Yeah, well what type aircraft is that?

A United DC-8

And what, and what's his altitude?

He was last cleared to five thousand.

Oh boy, our man was at five, too. We lost one aircraft. I don't know where he's at now.

Uh, La Guardia

Yeah

Uh, we haven't been able to, I haven't identified, ah, United yet.

Yeah, well we—he's going right over our approach course, this one target; he's coming up on our outer marker now.

Oh, I see, the one just coming up on your outer marker?

That's correct. We don't know who he is.

Okay, ah, just a minute. In the background, the Idlewild controller could be heard asking his colleague: *"Did you identify United yet, Pete? No, he's coming up on the outer marker. Yeah."*

LaGuardia approach control now contacted Newark tower to see if they had any information about the unknown plane that was now over Flatbush.

Newark, La Guardia, do you read? Idlewild, hang up. Newark, LaGuardia.

Newark Tower

Newark, this is LaGuardia

Yes?

Did you have any aircraft recently come from Preston heading up to our localizer?

No, we didn't, La Guardia

You didn't?

Nope, nothing that we're not working.

Okay, right.

LaGuardia Approach Control spoke now to their Tower.

Hey, Joe, we might have a mid-air collision, so, Walt's going up to alert the emergency equipment. It's TWA Two Sixty Six.

What's he, from Preston?

That's ah, he was coming from Linden, going down.

Okay, Steve.

At 10:39 a.m. the Idlewild Approach Center queried the New York control center to see if they perhaps were still tracking and directing the United jet.

New York are you by chance working United eight twenty-six?

United eighty twenty-six? Negative.

All right, we lost communications with him. We believe he's over the Idlewild VOR. We're not sure.
Hold it just a minute
New York.
Yeah?
Stand by. We just got a call from... ah... got a report from Newark that... ah... a plane...ah...went in just east of Staten Island in the water—a four-engine aircraft.

The United jet was flying straight and level when it struck the TWA Constellation, which was, at the moment of impact in a 22-degree left bank. When the United jet slammed into the Constellation, it almost severed the plane in half at its right rear quarter. A passenger seated in the center of the plane was sucked into one of the jet's massive engines. An explosion and fire erupted, and the plane began descending in a slow right turn. Though the TWA plane was shedding parts, it was still mostly intact. It made almost a complete 180 degree turn which had it now heading south in the direction of Miller Army Air Field on Staten Island. Over Miller Field, the Constellation once again exploded— most likely a fuel tank on the right wing. The plane then broke into four main parts: the tail section separated from the forward portion of the aircraft, the right vertical stabilizer and twelve feet of the right horizontal stabilizer were torn free and caught fire, the right wing and number four engine separated from the plane and exploded on fire, the number three engine and nacelle detached from the plane, the forward section and most of the wing and landing gear fell near the northwest corner of Miller Field. Numerous pieces of the Constellation were strewn over a wide area in the vicinity of Miller Air Field in New Dorp, Staten Island. Many pieces of the DC-8 were also strewn across the field, mingling with the Constellation's debris.

The United DC-8, despite the damage it sustained, remained airborne and headed toward Brooklyn.

7

Staten Island florist Paul Kleinau stood outside his shop, looking up at the sky overhead. He was happy to see the sky finally clearing and the sun coming out and wondered if the weather had cleared enough for him to put out some Christmas wreaths on display outside his shop. Then, suddenly he saw two planes collide in the brightening sky. The jet seemed to be attacking the smaller prop plane, "like a big shark." He couldn't believe he had just seen two planes collide in mid-air. He panicked and screamed, "Oh my God!" [12]

Milkman Edward McGairy, was standing outside his house thinking about putting Christmas lights on his tree when he heard a loud boom. Looking up he saw a huge orange ball of fire. Then he saw the Constellation spiraling down, like a wounded bird. Later, near his house, he found a suit coat. The right arm had been torn off and shoulder was stained red. A half-smoked pack of cigarettes was still in one pocket.

New Dorp, Staten Island resident Mrs. George Weber was in her kitchen making cookies with her niece when she heard a loud roar. "Listen to the thunder," she remarked to her niece. They went to the window, looked out, and saw a tremendous ball of fire about a mile off in the distance. As they watched the awful scene unfold before their eyes, they could see it was a plane. It seemed to fall a few feet before there was another loud bang and a huge burst of fire. One wing now gone, the plane continued to fall, turning over and over, spiraling down engulfed in a bright red flame. [13]

Mrs. Jacqueline Peacock was in the kitchen of her New Dorp home across from Miller Field when her house shook. She ran out onto her front porch, still in her pajamas. Metal and bits of leather were falling all around. When the plane fell at the far end of the field, she couldn't see very well but she did hear a terrible crashing sound, "as though someone dropped thousands of dishes from the sky." Bits of debris from the planes fell all over her yard and sidewalk. She noticed a piece of white material stuck in a tree. It looked like a towel or tablecloth, and it was stained red with blood. [14]

Most of the Staten Island observers of the falling TWA plane mentioned the sickening horror of the slow earthward spiraling of the fuselage that they knew contained the plane's passengers. They watched in horror as hundreds of airplane pieces began dropping over an area of eight or ten blocks.

Oil deliveryman Clifford Beuth saw the first engine on the right side blow up, followed by the second. As it did, the explosion blew the tail section to pieces. Beuth saw two people fall out of the plane as it whirled to the ground on fire. Residents ran from the streets to seek shelter from the fragments of metal and flaming debris that were raining down on their community. "I prayed that it would be over soon," said Frank Griffo, operator of a service station at New Dorp Lane and Hylan Boulevard. [15]

Twisted and burned shards of stainless steel weighing as much as fifty pounds slammed onto Staten Island's Hylan Boulevard and fell into yards and driveways. The debris narrowly missed a community of wooden homes and a public school. The flaming forward section of the craft smashed to earth on the northwest corner of Miller Army Air Field, less than 150 feet from the eight-room frame home of Edward Brody, on Boundary Lane. "I saw it coming right at us," Mrs. Brody said. "I ran upstairs to get my daughters, Cathy and Eileen. Then it stopped." A thirty-foot wing section and one engine swirled out of the overcast fifty feet from a row of frame officers' quarters at the field. Mrs. John Barry, whose husband was a chief warrant officer at Fort Wadsworth, picked up her 6-month-old daughter and ran out of her house into the heavy snow. The rear half of the fuselage spun to earth 100 yards from her home and split apart. About 1000 students were in classes at

Public School 41, two blocks away. Debris landed in the school yard but the students and the school were spared any damage. [16]

One of the engines from the United jet plummeted to earth fifteen blocks northwest of Miller Field, behind a housing development at Jefferson Street and Dongan Hills Road. It dug a crater four feet deep, nine feet wide, and twelve feet long. About 500 yards from the engine were portions of the outboard right wing section of the DC-8 and a part of the right aileron.

It was 10:33 a.m. and Army Sgt Glenn F. Logsdon, air traffic controller at Miller Field, suddenly saw a huge orange glow in the overcast sky. Then he saw the TWA Connie drop onto the field in three separate pieces. As bits of the aircraft rained from the sky onto Miller Field before his eyes, Logsdon hit all possible crash and emergency buttons, alerting civilian and governmental emergency services.

Frank Maybury, Staten Island dispatcher for Transit Authority buses, was in his radio car at New Dorp Lane and Hylan Boulevard. when he heard a noise that sounded like a jet breaking the sound barrier. Picking up a policeman, they both headed for Miller Field where they saw the plane go down. Maybury radioed his bus terminal to get police, fire and other emergency apparatus rolling. Then the two men engaged in the grim task of picking up parts of the bodies that had fallen on Hylan Boulevard. At Miller Field they also helped gather more body parts from the snow that was red with blood.

Two off-duty patrolmen, brothers Peter and Gerald Paul, were buying Christmas gifts at a New Dorp shopping center south of Miller Field. When they heard the crash, they left their packages in the store and raced to the field. With a small ladder they scaled the ten-foot cyclone fence topped with barbed wire and, along with Army Lieutenant Edward Monroe, who had joined them, rushed to the smoking rear section of the plane. They were the first ones there. Looking over a portion of the plane debris where bodies lay still strapped to their seats, they noted how deathly quiet it was. There was a lot of smoke and the seats were on fire. Peter spotted a man lying on his back in the snow and trying to get up. Taking out a knife, he began to cut people free from their seat belts. He counted nine passengers, only three of which were alive—two men and a woman. While the woman remained unidentified, the men were TWA passengers Robert McEachern and James Horsey.[17] McEachern, 22 years old, was from Cass City Michigan. He was first year law student at Ohio State University on his way to his parents' home to spend the Christmas holiday. Rescued by Coast Guard helo, he died after arrival at a hospital. The other man, 30-year-old James Horsey, of Front Royal, Virginia, was employed by the Riverton (Virginia) Lime and Stone company. He also died shortly after arriving at the hospital, succumbing to the serious injuries he had sustained. The other bodies were badly burned. Peter and Gerald Paul helped carry the victims to waiting helicopters for transport to the U. S. Public Health Service Hospital in St. George.

Dr. Ernest Siegfried of the Public Health Service Hospital also responded to the first emergency call. At the crash site, he witnessed what was, to him "nothing but a mass of rubble and human bodies." He watched as an Army tow truck pulled back a huge curved side of aluminum, and exposed many bodies, strapped in their seats, crushed and crumpled together. All their clothes were burned off. [18]

New York City fireman Frank Reinhold, who lived near Miller Field, was home at the time of the crash. He was playing with his two-year-old son, Jimmy, when he heard an explosion and his wife screamed, "There's a plane on fire!" Running to the rear door of his house, he saw a wing floating down through the air toward the water. He ran to the street, and, hitching a ride with a passing motorist, went to the crash site to see what he could do to help. When he arrived, he saw at least six bodies lying in the snow. [19]

Arthur Mazza, a 28-year-old firefighter assigned to Engine 159 on Staten Island raced out to Miller Field when the call came in. As Engine 159's trucks pulled up on Hylan Boulevard the firemen cut a hole in the fence surrounding the field to gain access. When Mazza neared the scene, he saw smoke billowing from between the trees and two bodies lying naked and broken in a wide red circle in the snow. Then he saw what was left of the TWA Constellation: five-foot-high piles of mangled metal, bodies-- some still in their seats, seatbelts fastened-- and luggage. Firemen quickly doused the smoldering wreckage with foam.

Miller Airfield was a cacophony of sound and confusion. Two-way radios crackled and sirens blared as fire trucks and ambulances rushed to the crash site. The emergency vehicles and the cars of local officials, turned the snow on the field into a muddy slush.

Jim Romano, a Daily News photographer, followed Mazza's Engine 159 truck to the scene. He was one of the first journalists to arrive and security had not been set up. He roamed freely, photographing the destruction. He photographed the crushed cockpit with the pilot and copilot visible inside. One of them still had a cigarette in his hand.

At 10:34 a.m., Supervising Dispatcher Anthony Lauritis at Fire Headquarters, Staten Island, received an alarm from a box at Lincoln Avenue and Grand Place, and transmitted it to other firehouses. Seconds later, eight more fire boxes in the Staten Island neighborhood rang in and the switchboard lit up with 30 telephone calls reporting that a plane had crashed at Miller Field. Lauritis wasn't too alarmed. It was a small military field used mostly for single-engine aircraft. He figured two pumpers and two ladder trucks could handle it. He was wrong. [20] Chief Roger Carmody of the Eighth Division arrived at the scene, took one look, and ordered a second alarm, bringing four more pumpers, four extra ladder trucks, and police and fire rescue squads.

Some of the first rescuers at the Staten Island crash were artillery men and aircraft maintenance men stationed at Miller Field. Lieutenant Victor Boner, provost marshal, came from Fort Wadsworth, to take charge. Assistant Chief Inspector Walter Klotzbach directed 150 cops on the scene, and additional help was rushed from the fort, including 100 soldiers.

The first fire trucks reached the scene within three minutes of getting the call. Firemen cut their way through the wire fence surrounding the field with clippers and ran hose lines to the fiercely burning forward section while foam tanks smothered the blaze from the engines. Two alarms brought 100 firemen to the scene. Seventy-five off-duty men responded as well. Within minutes the fire was out and the smoking wreckage was being pulled apart by winches and crowbars.

A group of firemen chopped open the cockpit with an ax and removed the bodies of the pilot, David Wollam, and copilot, Dean Bowen. Mrs. Bowen at her Long Island home with her two young children was notified by TWA officials of the crash. They advised her against going out to the crash scene, telling her she would just be sitting in traffic and wouldn't be available to get a call from the hospital if it should come in. She took their advice but was haunted by images of her husband lying helpless in the snow.[21]

The firemen lifted out body after body. These they placed in even rows in the snow, covered by olive drab Army blankets brought by soldiers from the quarters at the far end of the field. There they waited for their eventual removal to New York's Bellevue Hospital morgue. Ambulances arrived from all over the island. Bellevue Hospital disaster units made the trip by ferry. Five priests from St. Charles Roman Catholic Seminary nearby and the

Rev. John J. Lennon of Our Lady Queen of Peace Roman Catholic Church in New Dorp, knelt beside the dead to administer last rites.

Because debris littered the Lower Bay off New Dorp, it was feared some plane victims might be in the water. So, the Coast Guard dispatched a helicopter from Floyd Bennett Field in Brooklyn and 25 boats, from forty-foot picket launches to 180-footers, with a total of 200 men aboard them. They searched the water in vain from 11 a.m. until darkness fell. Four police launches, with fifteen men aboard, joined the futile search. No one was in the water, and no survivors were found.

As morning turned to afternoon, the skies above Staten Island, though still grey and dreary, began to clear, showing now and then a glimpse of sunlight. Outside the wire barriers of Miller Army Air Field, adults and children stood silently where they had gathered to watch the rescue efforts and try to make some sense of the tragedy whose aftermath they were witnessing.

Inside the fence, the work went on. Plastic sacks of mail were removed from the forward section of the plane. The plane's log books and documents were impounded. A patrolman found a .38 caliber revolver in the snow. A line of soldiers was formed at the east end of the 50-acre field. Walking a yard or so apart, they combed every inch of the snow-covered field for pieces of the plane or human remains that had not yet been gathered.

Red Cross and Salvation Army canteens handed out hot coffee to the rescuers.

The Plainfield office of New Jersey Bell Telephone Company sent a crew of six men to Miller Field, to set up an emergency field communications unit. Wires were strung several thousand feet to roads bordering the field.

Over several miles across the New Dorp area of Staten Island was scattered the all too human evidence of the tragedy that had just occurred. A woman's blouse dangled from a branch. Bits of foam rubber hung like confetti from the trees. An overnight case, its edges singed, with baby pants and a nightgown lay haphazardly in the slushy field. There was a checkbook, flipped open, in the snow. It showed a balance of $3.48. There was one shoe, its knot still neatly tied, its polish still shining. There was a rosary and a religious book with the Virgin Mother on the cover. There were, in many places, bits and pieces of Christmas packages.[22]

At 2 p.m., the sun finally came out. It glinted off the almost undamaged triple tail rudder of what was left of Constellation No. 907 N6907C bound from Ohio that, with its five crew members and 39 passengers, had never reached its destination.

8

The Park Slope neighborhood of Brooklyn is two blocks south of busy Flatbush Avenue and about half a mile northwest and down the hill from Prospect Park. In 1960, it was a neighborhood in transition. Once spacious apartments had been divided into smaller units and many of the brownstones became rooming houses as lower income families of primarily Irish and Italian descent began moving in. But it was a close-knit neighborhood where small businesses thrived on the street level of the tenements while the business owners lived above and other families occupied the apartments on the upper levels. Everyone knew everyone else and, in the summer, people sat on their stoops in front of the tenements chatting, drinking beer, and watching their children play in the street. [23]

On December 16, the windows of the businesses and residences were adorned for Christmas with garlands, wreaths, and other festive decorations. Trash barrels, their collection delayed by the snow storm earlier in the week, waited for the sanitation workers to come by and empty them.

John Opperisano and his nephew Joseph Colacano were selling Christmas trees on Sterling Place. Only six years apart in age the two men were more like brothers than uncle and nephew, and they had grown up together. Charles Cooper, a 34-year-old sanitation worker was clearing snow from the public sidewalk on Sterling and dentist, Dr. Jacob Crooks was walking his cocker spaniel Terry, which Dr. Crooks had gotten as a puppy. His faithful companion for many years, Terry was old as dogs go—upward of 12 and beginning to fail. But he always enjoyed a walk with his master, even on the cold and snowy streets of Brooklyn. As long as they were together, both man and dog were happy.

Children were in school—one of the first days this week, having had their schedules cut short by the early winter snowfall earlier in the week. Adults were off to work, or shopping, or running errands. Housewives were having a second morning cup of coffee, and listened to the radio or TV as they went about their household chores.

Shortly after 10:30 am, the neighborhood was jarred to a frightened standstill as a loud roar, and the sight of a huge jetliner flying low overhead broke the morning stillness.

It was United 826.

After colliding with the TWA Constellation over Staten Island, the crippled airliner, missing an engine, part of its right wing, and part of the leading edge of its left wing, remained airborne. It continued flying in a northeasterly direction, across the Narrows of the New York Bay and into Brooklyn. It travelled approximately eight and a half miles from the point of the collision before it came crashing down in the Park Slope neighborhood of Brooklyn, at the intersection of Sterling Place and 7th Avenue.

Captain Sawyer and First Officer Fiebing undoubtedly tried everything they could to regain some control of the aircraft after the collision, but there was too much damage. They couldn't control the jet's altitude and probably could not control its direction, as it continued to descend at 200 mph. When it reached Sterling Place, between 6th and 7th Avenues, the left wing of the jet struck the top of 126 Sterling Place, leaving a 15-foot section embedded in the building, with two feet of the wing protruding from the roof. The contact of the left wing with the building caused the jet to pivot sharply to the left. Slamming into the steeply gabled roof of the Pillar of Fire Church across the street, the thirty-foot tail section tore off, landing grotesquely askew in the intersection of Sterling Place and Seventh Avenue, its tip resting atop the cab of Roy Rothenberg's box rental truck. The rest of the plane came apart as it made contact with the ground and exploded in a series of fiery blasts igniting roofs and spraying debris over a wide area.

The rear section of the passenger cabin impacted the ground and slid, coming to rest facing in a northerly direction on Sterling Place. The flight deck crashed into the same area and burst into flames. The left wing, except for the outer fifteen feet that was embedded in the roof of the four-story building at 126 Sterling Place, came to rest in the intersection of the two streets.

Women, children, and elderly people came pouring out of the buildings into the street, dressed in housecoats, sweaters, and pajamas. They ran panic-stricken from the smoldering wreckage. The section of the left wing that had landed atop 126 Sterling Place, set fire to the roof. The fire spread to similar structures at 122, 120, and 118 Sterling Place, on the south side of the street. In its descent, the jet also ignited six buildings on Seventh Avenue.

At 119 Sterling Place, the Pillar of Fire Church, a 2 ½ story brick structure, suffered a direct hit, and the explosions that followed dug a 25-foot deep crater, some 50 feet in diameter. The body of the church's 90-year-old caretaker, Wallace Lewis, was found in the rubble of the church.

Next to the burning church, a five-story tenement stood gutted by fire. Next door, at the northwest corner of Seventh Avenue, flames poured steadily from the roof of the red-brick McCaddin funeral home.

In the third-floor living quarters above the funeral home, Henry McCaddin and his wife, Pauline, were having a mid-morning cup of coffee. Their one-year-old daughter, Donna Marie was playing under the kitchen table. Hearing the sound of a jet engine disturbingly close, Pauline said to her husband, "My goodness, that plane sounds awfully low!" Just then the whole house shook like it had been hit by a bomb, and the room was all flames. Mrs.

McCaddin started to grab her daughter when their neighbor, Robert Carter, who had seen flames coming from the McCaddin's residence, rushed in. Pauline tossed the baby down the stairs into her neighbor's arms. They all ran out of the building. Carter later tried to get near the plane to see if he could help but the fire was so intense, it singed his eyebrows and pushed him back.[24] [25]

Across Sterling Place from McCaddin's, a Chinese laundry and a delicatessen were sideswiped by the burning fuselage and caught fire. The laundry's owner, James Moy, known in the neighborhood as "Jimmy the Laundryman", was in the front of his shop ironing a shirt when the plane hit. He was able to reach the street only slightly singed.

Nick Ligelis owned a flower shop at 312 Flatbush Avenue. He and his daughter, Constance Ciazzo, saw "some very horrible things" from a window of the shop, near the crash scene. Nick saw a plane fall directly on top of some automobiles outside his store. He knew there were people in them. He heard screaming from the ensuing smoke and flames. Constance saw a boy, 17 or 18 years old, running from the accident, his face covered with blood, his eyes bulging wide. He was screaming, 'Oh, those people are burning to death!' Her husband grabbed the boy and shook him but he kept running. [26]

Brooklyn accountant William Noble and his wife were working on a set of books when they heard a tremendous crash. Then the wall caved in, throwing Mrs. Noble into her husband. They scrambled from the building.

At the intersection of Sterling Place and Seventh Avenue, Salvatore Manza, a Department of Sanitation worker was shoveling snow when he heard a whistling sound. Looking up, he saw a plane, not even fifty feet up. It was coming down quickly. All of a sudden, the left wing dipped. It hooked into the corner of an apartment house roof, and the rest of the plane slammed into the church and the apartment house across the street. All at once everything was on fire, and the fire from the plane in the street was as high as the houses. Manza and another sanitation worker ran to the aid of their coworker Charles Cooper, but Cooper was already dead. Though he was seriously burned, they identified their friend by the peculiar way he had of tying his shoelaces.[27]

George Burch, was watching television just around the corner when he heard a huge noise that threw him out of his chair. Grabbing his window blinds to look out, he saw a mailman lying in the gutter. John Senator had been literally knocked for a loop. The impact of the crash caused him to do a complete somersault in the snow. First he was on his feet, then he wasn't, then he was. Burch put on a pair of pants and ran out of the building in his bare feet. Senator got up, then collapsed again, then got up again. Once Burch was certain the mailman was all right, he ran back in his apartment and put on his shoes and socks. He ran toward the crash scene but couldn't get closer because of the heat and the smoke.

The Reverend Raymond Morgan, a Catholic priest, was walking down the street in the area of 7th Avenue and Sterling Place, when he saw something that looked like a guided missile coming out of the sky. He ran to the corner and as he was running, he heard an explosion. Turning the corner, he saw a large flame that went skyward. Rev. Morgan ran into the rectory and told the other priests what had happened. He got some holy oil with the intent to administer the last rites, but as he approached the plane, the flames and heat were so tremendous, he was not able to get close; he could only look at the bodies in the debris.

Just as residents were running out of their homes and away from the crash site, sight-seers were rushing up to the scene from every side street and clogging up the roadways and sidewalks. The crowds impeded rescue efforts until the police ordered them away and roped off an area of sixteen city blocks. When rescuers were seen carrying bodies from the burning buildings, no one knew whether they were residents of the apartments or victims from the plane.

Joseph DiFrulo was 12 years old and in the 6th grade at St. Augustine's grammar school in the Park Slope neighborhood of Brooklyn. On the morning of December 16th, he didn't want to go to school and was trying to convince his mother to keep him home. If he could ever talk his mother into keeping him home, he loved to do it on a Friday. So, on this particular day, it was 8:30 in the morning and Joseph was pleading his case.

"I really don't want to go to school. I feel sick," he whined to his mother.

"No, Joseph you're going to school."

Joseph continued to plead with her, until finally she asked him, "Well, why don't you want to go to school?"

"Because it's boring. Nothing ever really happens."

"Well, what do you want to have happen?"

Joseph thought for a moment, what *did* he want to happen? He hadn't really given that a thought before. Finally, he blurted out, "Well maybe if a plane would crash."

"What an awful thing to say!" his mother rebuked him. "That's terrible. Get to school. Don't ever say a horrible thing like that again!"

Realizing he had lost the battle, Joseph set out for school. St Augustine's was nearby, only about three blocks away and it took him only about ten minutes to walk there.

His classroom was on the top floor of the school building and his younger sister, in the first grade, was on the first floor. He sat in the classroom around 10:30 on that Friday morning staring out the window. It was cloudy and there were snow flurries in the air. It was cold, but not bone-chillingly so. All in all, it was a dismal day.

All of a sudden, he heard the sound of a jet. The sound got louder and louder until it shook the whole building. He and the other students were stunned. This was so close and they were on the top floor. Within seconds there was a huge explosion and he knew the jet had crashed. And he knew something else, horribly disturbing: he just knew he had caused the plane to crash by what he had said to his mother just two hours ago. Joseph began crying, asking himself, "Oh, my God, what did I do?"

No one could leave the school, so they stayed in the classroom for some time. Eventually, the principal came over the PA system and gave the teachers instructions to take their classes down to the school's auditorium. There they set up a kind of staging area where the parents could come and claim their children and take them home.

Back at the DiFrulo house, Joseph's mother was on the phone talking to her father and knew nothing about what was going on even though they were only three blocks away. The only thing she heard were fire engines---she never heard the plane crash. All of a sudden out of nowhere, Joseph's father, who only worked a few blocks away on Flatbush Avenue, came bursting through the door. "Don't you know what's going on?!" he exclaimed.

"No, what's happening?"

"The school was hit by a plane!"

They rushed to the school to get Joseph and his sister. The only way out brought them within a block of where the plane had crashed. They could see everything was still burning. Police were everywhere, fire engines were everywhere and they could smell the jet plane fuel very heavy in the air.

At St. Augustine's High School, the 24-year old teacher, Brother Conrad Barnes' first clue that something was wrong was when he noticed a student near the window suddenly turn pale. He went to the window and saw the United jet flying low and descending toward the school. The plane was about 1,000 yards away and Brother Conrad was convinced they were going to be hit. But then he saw the plane bank precariously, it's wings almost vertical to the ground, as it swerved past the school. Several boys stood up and Brother Conrad told them to be still. He was afraid that the children would panic if he told them to evacuate and was thinking of telling them to put their heads on their desks and say a prayer when there was a tremendous impact. Rushing to the roof of the school, Brother Conrad saw flames shooting 50 to 75 feet above some nearby rooftops.[28]

The plane had mercifully missed hitting St. Augustine's Catholic School with its 1700 pupils inside. When the plane crashed at Sterling and 7th Avenue a block away, the school's superior took over the public-address system and led the students in recitation of the rosary for the victims of the crash.

At the Berkeley Institute, a private school in Brooklyn two blocks from Sterling and 7th Avenue, the children were busy exchanging gifts and cards and handing out holiday cookies and candy. The rooms were festively decorated with a tree and paper wreaths in the windows. Nancy Vrooman, who was serving as a student teacher was on her way to the school office to check on the ice cream for the second grade Christmas party when there was a loud noise followed by an explosion. The whole building shook. Children were thrown from their seats. Books flew off the shelves. A woman rushed into the school screaming, "Oh my God...Oh, my God.....there's been a plane crash. Get the children out of here!" Students were beginning to run into the office to find out what was going on. The headmistress, Helen Mason, grabbed her coat and hurried outside to see what was happening. What she saw was horrible. The United Airlines jet was lying in pieces in the street, fiercely burning. Some of the smoke began to seep into the school. Mrs. Mason told Nancy to get the kindergarteners and first graders from the building and next door to the gymnasium. The dazed and confused youngsters followed her orders. As the students sat on the floor in the gym, they began to complain and ask questions. "Why aren't we having our Christmas party?" one little boy complained. "I'm hungry," another child shouted. Mrs. Mason asked the children to be calm and cooperate. Then she told them what had happened. The children became deathly quiet. Both teachers and students were scared, not knowing what was going to happen next. Outside the smoke had turned the sky dark black and they could smell its acrid odor as it seeped into the building despite the tightly closed doors and windows. Nancy went back to the classrooms to make sure no children had been left behind. The rooms were quiet. On the desks sat the cookies and candy, and the now melting ice cream. The lighted Christmas tree stood alone in the corner. Before long, frantic mothers began to come for their children, guiding them safely home.[29]

Roy Rothenberg had rented a truck that day to make a pickup at a manufacturing company in South Brooklyn. When he came to a stop sign at the corner of 7th and Sterling Place there was a tremendous explosion followed by a ball of fire rising up right in front of him. He didn't even know what it was until much later. He ducked under the instrument panel until the flames died a little, then he got out of the truck and ran back toward Flatbush Avenue. The entire tail section of the plane snapped off and came to rest in the middle of the intersection. The tip of the tail touched the forward cargo section of Rothenberg's truck and cracked the windshield. He miraculously escaped without a scratch.

Johnny Marotta and his friend Jimmy had pulled up behind Rothenberg's truck just after the crash and Rothenberg's escape from the vehicle. They hadn't seen the plane crash. For some reason they did not see or did not remember the explosion and the flames. All Johnny remembered was finding no one in the stopped truck that was blocking their way through the intersection and seeing the tail of the plane resting gently on the forward cargo wall of the rental truck.

When Johnny returned to the car and told Jimmy there was "a friggin' plane in the street," Jimmy said, "You're crazy" and got out of the car to see for himself. When he came back to the car he was pale with shock at what he had seen. "I gotta get the car out," he said. Johnny told him to go ahead, but he wanted to go see about the people in the Ford he had seen on the 7th Avenue side of the intersection. The tail of the plane was pinning it down. When he got to the car, it was full of black smoke. Johnny tried to open the doors. He went around to all four doors but they were all locked, so he tried to break out a window. Meanwhile, eight or ten people had gathered at the intersection and began pounding on the glass trying to break the windows with no success. Finally, someone picked up a brick or a stone from the street and broke out a window. Reaching in, they unlocked the door. The smoke came billowing out, but there was no one in the car. Later, Johnny surmised what must have happened. It was a Brooklyn thing, but you always lock your car. You never leave anything open in Brooklyn. He figured that whoever had been inside, despite what had happened, had the wherewithal to lock the doors as they escaped from the car.

Johnny could see the flames coming from the street and the surrounding tenements. He and several other bystanders started up the street toward the flaming buildings. But their progress was stopped by explosion after explosion as the gas tanks of parked cars along Sterling Place ignited from the heat of the flames and the jet fuel and blew up. It was like a macabre dance, as Johnny and the others took two steps toward the burning wreckage and were forced one step back by an exploding automobile.

Priests from St. Augustine's ran to the scene with Holy Oils. They found the intersection ablaze with jet fuel and exploding automobiles. The heat was terrific and the flames were shooting three stories high. They could hear no screams coming from the plane, and the heat from the fires kept the priests from getting anywhere near it, so they helped people get out of threatened houses.

About a hundred refugees from burned-out tenements were sheltered and fed by civil defense units at Public School 9, on Sterling Place and Vanderbilt Avenue, and at St. Augustine's Roman Catholic School. Red Cross workers set up a shelter and canteen within half an hour in the Carlton movie theatre at Flatbush Avenue and Seventh Avenue. The Red Cross also brought in 400 pints of blood, with 200 more close by. Within fifteen minutes after the crash, the Salvation Army doughnut and coffee truck was ready to feed rescue workers in Brooklyn. Food carts of the Red Cross and the Three Alarm Association arrived only a little later. Boy Scouts of Troop 22, attached to St. Francis Xavier Roman Catholic Church in Brooklyn, served as runners for civil defense workers in Brooklyn.

New York Mayor Robert F. Wagner hastened to Brooklyn and sent his executive secretary, Frank Doyle, to Staten Island. New York Fire Commissioner Edward J. Cavanagh, was being interviewed on a radio program when he heard of the crash. He cut the interview short and rushed to the scene and remained there until late into the night directing operations. Police Commissioner Stephen P. Kennedy also hurried to the scene. He implored all persons in the New York metropolitan area to keep away from the disaster scenes so they would not hamper emergency crews but many ignored his plea. From Washington, the American Red Cross dispatched its national director of disaster services, Enzo Bighinatti, to New York and from Dayton came Elwood R. Quesada, administrator of the Federal Aviation Agency, to join in the investigation of the tragedy. Ironically Quesada had been in Dayton to commemorate the Dec 17 anniversary of the Wright Brothers first flight.

Police diverted all southbound traffic on Flatbush Avenue to St. Marks Avenue, three blocks from the scene. Flatbush Avenue, from Bergen Street to Prospect Park, was closed to all but emergency equipment. The Brooklyn-Manhattan Battery Tunnel was closed to regular auto traffic to permit speedy movement of emergency equipment. The Brooklyn bound lanes of the Manhattan Bridge also were closed to all but emergency apparatus.

All supplies of gas and electricity in an eight-block area were shut off to prevent further fires.

At Brooklyn Fire Alarm Headquarters, Supervising Dispatcher Robert Johnson, already had heard of the Staten Island crash just as Alarm Box 1231 rang in at 10:36 a.m. from Seventh Avenue and Sterling Place. Even as the alarm was going out to the fire houses, two more boxes in the neighborhood sounded, and eighteen callers were on the telephone to Johnson and his eight assistants.

At 10:39 am, Chief John A. Panarello of the 48th Battalion arrived at the Brooklyn crash scene. Just like the firefighters on Staten Island, the Brooklyn firefighters thought at first that the crash involved a small, propeller plane and the number of crash victims would be small, but, as with the Staten Island responders, when Panarello saw what they were dealing with, he ordered a second alarm. Five minutes later, a third alarm was called. The chief called the fourth alarm at 10:46 for Rescue Squad No. 1 from Manhattan. At 10:50 the 5th alarm was transmitted, then a sixth and the seventh sending all the units assigned to a second alarm at Box 174 in Manhattan to the scene.

Engine 269 and Ladder 105 were the first New York Fire Department companies to arrive on the scene. When they got there, they found themselves faced with jet fuel fed fires raging in ten brownstones, a five-story brick apartment building filled with fire and in danger of collapse, the Pillar of Fire Church in flames, and the intersection and nearby streets filled with burning debris from what had once been the United jet.

Along Sterling Place about four feet of ice-encrusted snow was piled up where it had been shoveled from the snowstorm earlier in the week. The snow banks were obscuring the fire hydrants. Johnny Marotta, fellow bystanders, and first responders lined up along the sidewalk and began to dig through the snow with their hands trying to find a fireplug. A fireman finally came along with a shovel and dug out the hydrants.

Once the hydrants were located and dug out, Engine 269 stretched a line to the southwest corner of Seventh Avenue and Sterling Place. Ladder 105 rolled up and Lt. James Bush split his company into two teams. He ordered Firemen John Rogan and John Dailey to attempt the rescue of passengers, several of whom they could see strapped to their seats as flames closed in. Equipped with only fire extinguishers carried to the scene by civilians, the firemen approached the flaming wreckage, braving extreme heat from the burning jet fuel. As Dailey directed the extinguishers, Rogan was able cut away the seat belts of two passengers who were pulled from the burning plane. The firemen wore heavy canvas gloves to shield their hands from the hot and jagged metal. It wasn't long before they were driven back by an overwhelming wall of flames and were unable to return. [30]

Once the flames were brought under control and no longer a threat, firemen once again waded through the debris to retrieve what bodies they could find. In many cases, all they found were pieces. An arm, a leg, or a completely blackened and charred body.

Firemen waded through ankle-deep water and stepped over piles of snow and ice to carry body after body to temporary morgues in two garages. The procession of the olive drab stretchers continued while other firemen removed charred mail and documents from the wreckage. [31]

Bodies were removed at the rate of ten an hour to temporary morgues, set up in a garage next to the demolished Pillar of Fire Church and in a bowling alley on Seventh Ave., near Flatbush. Some rescuers carried out the dead in canvas sacks laced with clothesline, four rescuers to a stretcher. A fleet of city mortuary trucks stood by at Park Place and Seventh Avenue in Brooklyn. Three hours after the United Airliner crashed, only a couple dozen of the dead had been removed. Dozens more remained to be found.

Johnny Marotta stood with others on the corner of Sterling and 7th Avenue, unable to leave, lest they feel they had abandoned any hope of being able to help somehow. He knew his mother would be worried and wondering why he wasn't home yet, but he felt he couldn't leave. He was a part of this now. He watched the firemen and other first responders running, carrying stretchers with human remains from the crash. In front of the buildings at the northeast corner of 7th and Sterling, was a concrete wall topped with wrought iron decorative spikes, about two feet high. As firemen rushed toward the corner carrying a body, Johnny watched in horror as the firemen ran into the wall, and one man fell, impaling himself on the iron spikes of the wall. The men dropped the body they were carrying as the others freed their fellow fire fighter from the spikes.

After the fire from the plane was put out, the firemen went to work on the tenements. They hoisted ladders to bring their hoses onto the upper stories where pieces of the jet had smashed through walls and burned holes in the floors below. The scene was described by Paul Hashagen in his book "Stories of Fire" :

"Lt. Bush and Fireman John J. Browne Jr. hurried to 26 Seventh Avenue, a heavily damaged five-story brick tenement. A wing and two of the United plane's engines were found in front of it. The firemen found the first and fifth floors heavily involved in fire, and the exterior side and rear of the building also in flames. Despite the imminent danger of collapse, they entered the flaming building with no hoselines for protection. Amidst the waves of heat and pulsing smoke they searched. On the fourth floor Browne found a crippled elderly woman. With great difficulty he managed to carry her down to the third floor but was too exhausted to continue. Lt. Bush heard his call for assistance and made his way to the third floor. Together they were able to remove the woman to safety and turned her over to an ambulance crew."[32]

In other areas, firemen dropped their hoses and began a search of the tangle of wooden beams, airplane parts, and ripped up walls and ceilings. They trudged into the mess, and with bare hands, tossed debris behind them as they worked forward searching for injured residents.

In his butcher shop at 138 Sterling Place, Albert Layer had been working at getting cuts of meat ready for his afternoon customers when the United jet crashed on the street outside his shop. At home, Layer's son, off-duty Fireman William Layer attached to Hook and Ladder Co. 159, heard radio bulletins on the crash. He picked up his helmet, boots and rubber fireman's coat and raced to the scene. He helped as water was poured by the ton into the flaming ruins of his father's shop. He kept anxiously scanning the faces of the curious crowds which had gathered. Nowhere was his father to be seen. He carried on his duties, trying hard not to think about his father. He would have to worry about him later.

As Johnny Marotta stood on the eastern side of Sterling Avenue, he was separated from the other side of the street by the smoldering wreckage of the airliner. He couldn't cross the street, but that did not prevent him from viewing what was happening there. On the northwest corner of Sterling and 7th was a three-story brownstone building, and there he saw an elderly woman, dressed only in a white peignoir standing precariously on a third story ledge outside her partially destroyed building, screaming for help. He could hear the bystanders on the sidewalk below the woman, and heard them calling to her, but with all the noise and tumult around him, he couldn't tell if they were calling for her to "jump" or "don't jump." He stood for a moment mesmerized. Even with all the chaos and horror that was going on around him, the vision of this woman standing on the ledge, calling for help, transfixed him. Her long grey hair and her white silken nightgown flowed in the breeze. She didn't have her peignoir buttoned and as the wind picked it up, it looked to Johnny like the woman had wings, like an angel. The last vision he had of her was her leaning over and falling, but he wasn't sure if what he was seeing was really happening. He never saw or learned what actually happened to her. Perhaps she fell. Perhaps she was saved by a fireman or bystanders. That one picture was to haunt him the rest of his life.

By 12:43, Chief of Department George David was able to declare the Brooklyn fire under control. By 1:30 pm, most of the flames in the 11 affected structures finally had been doused.

As dusk fell on the city, and darkness overspread the neighborhood that looked like a war-torn city, police, firemen, and civilians continued the backbreaking and heartbreaking work of scouring the plane's wreckage for bodies and the smoldering tenements for any residents injured and left behind. As night began to fall, the Fire Department put its emergency searchlight units into action, bathing the scene in an eerie white light. In the glare, hundreds of firemen continued to search the rubble turning up bits of evidence to help identify the victims. Only small telltale signs of the lives that had cheerfully boarded the United flight a few hours before remained strewn in the street: a man's shoe, stuck in the dirty snow near the remains of the passenger cabin; a little baby's romping harness, unmarked by the crash or fire, and with no name on its brass tag—just a shipping ticket.

In total, seven alarms and borough calls were transmitted, bringing fifty fire companies with 200 firemen to the scene. There were 31 engine companies, six ladder companies, three rescue companies and four special units. They were joined by almost two hundred off-duty firefighters who'd responded on their own. Robert Condon, the city's Civil Defense Director, turned on a citywide disaster signal and 500 men and women civilians—trained as auxiliary policemen, firemen, first-aid men, drivers, messengers, nurses—responded to the scenes of the two crashes. The city's Hospital Department had dispatched every available ambulance, doctor, and nurse in both municipal and private hospitals to both the Brooklyn and the Staten Island crash scenes, including disaster units from Bellevue and Kings County Hospitals. Kings County Hospital sent four ambulances, twenty doctors, eight nurses, and eight attendants to the Brooklyn scene. Bellevue Hospital's similar disaster unit went first to Staten Island and then to Brooklyn. A score of city and voluntary hospitals in Brooklyn also sent ambulances, doctors, and nurses to Sterling Place. The only people they found requiring medical attention were rescuers and first responders who injured themselves in their efforts to search the wreckage, carry bodies, and aide the residents who had run from their burning tenements.

Sanitation worker Charles Cooper, Pillar of Fire church caretaker Wallace Lewis, the Christmas tree salesmen, John Opperisano and Joseph Colacano, and the butcher Albert Layer were found dead. Dr. Crooks was found badly burned on the sidewalk, his dog nowhere to be found. He was taken to the hospital but later died from his injuries. Crooks was the last person to die in the tragedy.

There were no survivors from the United plane---except one.

9

Aboard the United DC-8, eleven-year old Stephen Baltz sat gazing out the window at the landscape below as the plane descended over New York. The ground was still snow-covered and he thought it looked just like a fairyland. Then there was an explosion, and people began screaming. The next thing he knew, he was thrown from the plane, the little gray suit he had donned so happily just that morning on fire. When he opened his eyes and looked up and saw four policemen, staring down at him. A man and a woman knelt by his side. The woman was holding an umbrella over him, protecting him from the light snow that was gently falling.

The woman with the umbrella was Dorothy Fletcher who lived at 143 Berkeley Place, just down the street from Seventh Avenue at the time of the crash. The back of her apartment faced Sterling Place. She had called in sick to work that day from her job with a Manhattan chemical company and was in her kitchen when she heard a plane flying low over her apartment. She immediately thought, "That plane is in trouble." Then came the explosion and the flames shooting up as high as the rooftops of the surrounding brownstones. As a member of Civil Defense, she sprang into action, grabbing her coat and racing out.   As she turned on Seventh Avenue she saw the remnants of the plane she had just heard flying overhead strewn up and down the block, the tail resting at the intersection of Sterling Place and 7th Avenue.

When she got to the crash scene, she identified herself to a policeman.

"What can I do to help?" she asked.

"Take care of that little boy. He was a passenger," he told her.

Dorothy turned and saw a young boy—he looked to her to be between 8 and 10 years old--lying in a snowbank. His skin was so blackened by his burns, that at first, she thought he might be

African American. His jacket was still smoldering, but he was conscious and was talking. That was when she learned his name was Stephen. As she held her umbrella over him, Dorothy realized from her first aid training that the boy was in shock. She looked up at people who were hanging out the windows of the surrounding tenements and called to them, "Please throw me down a few blankets. He's in shock. I have to get him to the hospital. If he comes out of this, he'll be in agony." [33]

In a radio car, Patrolman Ralph Pica and Joseph Mannino of the Bergen St. station were cruising west on Sterling Place when they heard the explosion behind them about 100 yards away and drove back to the crash. Dorothy accosted the men inquiring of them if they had a car. The streets were so jammed with stalled automobile traffic ambulances were as yet unable to get through. She knew they had to get the boy to a hospital fast. The men laid Stephen in the back seat of the radio car. Kneeling beside him on the way to the hospital, Dorothy tried to keep the boy calm, but he wanted to talk. It nearly broke her heart when he looked up at her and asked, "Am I going to die?"

"Not if we can help it," she reassured him. She told him not to worry, that she had a son his age (although her son was actually 17) and knew he was going to be all right. [34]

"We're taking you to Methodist Hospital," she told him.

"That's good," he replied, "because I am a Methodist." Stephen told her that his father was still in Chicago and that his mother and sister were waiting for him at the airport. They were going to spend Christmas with his uncle up in Yonkers. [35] His only complaint was "My legs are so cold."

Stephen was still alert and responsive when he first arrived at the hospital. He reached into his pocket and pulled out a wallet. Handing it to one of the doctors he said, "My father's number is in there. Will you please call him?" The boy then told doctors: "I was looking out of the window at the city with everyone else, looking at all of the snow, and all of a sudden, there was an explosion and the plane was going down. That's all I remember." [36]

Meanwhile, at Idlewild Airport, Stephen's mother and sister were waiting for his plane. When the news of the crash came in, Mrs. Baltz, along with all the other families waiting for loved ones at the airport were in a panic of worry, sobbing, and hoping. When the news of her son's survival was given her, Mrs. Baltz broke into a great smile of joy. She left in a car for the hospital driven by a United Airlines representative. On the way, Stephen's sister, 9-year-old Randee, reassured her mother, "Don't worry, Mother, Stevie will be all right." [37] When Mrs. Baltz first saw her son, in spite of his obvious injuries, the bandages, and medical equipment surrounding him, she thought he was the most beautiful sight in the world. She repeatedly sobbed, "He's alive. He's alive." [38]

When he learned of the crash and the improbable survival of his young son, William Baltz, Sr. got on the next available plane from Chicago, landing in New York at 4:25 p.m. At the hospital, the boy's parents were given their own room near Stevie's while his sister, Randee was sent back to stay with her grandparents in New York. Baltz calmly leaned over his son and spoke to him as if nothing was wrong. Stephen looked up at him and said "Hello, Dad." He then asked his father if his wrist watch, which he had been wearing, had been damaged. But the watch on his wrist, crushed and smelling of jet fuel had been taken off his blood-smeared arm when he entered the hospital emergency room. It bore silent witness to the disaster--it was stopped at 9:37 Chicago time. His sense of humor still intact, Stephen told his father he wanted to be a pilot and fly the plane himself next time. [39]

Barbara Stull, a 21-year old nurse who had just recently graduated from nursing school had reported to Methodist Hospital when word of the disaster came in. She stayed until 6 pm, and as she was leaving she stopped at the security office to remind the nursing director that she would be back for her shift at midnight. Barbara walked over to the chapel for a minute to say a prayer for the victims of the crash, and the sole survivor—little Stephen Baltz. When she came out of the chapel, the nursing director told her: 'Barbara, we'll use you. You'll special him tonight.' " That meant one nurse for one patient. That terribly burned boy would be hers.

Stephen had been placed in a glassed-in private room on the fourth floor and when Barbara entered to begin her shift, he was surrounded by doctors, nurses, and equipment. When she first saw him, he was so badly burned, Barbara couldn't even tell what race he was. **Eighty per cent of Stephen's body had been burned and his left leg had been fractured. The most serious third-degree burns were on his chest and shoulders.** She saw a bone sticking out of one of his legs. The orthopedic doctors could not take the risk of resetting it because of the seriousness of his burns. He was covered only by a small, sterilized sheet on his groin. They could not cover the rest of his body with a sheet because of the risk of infection to his open wounds and his raw skin. **He was receiving fluid nourishment and blood plasma through an IV placed in his arm.**

The doctors gave Barbara a report of the boy's condition and what she could expect during the night. One by one they left, leaving Barbara, and two young nursing students to look after Stephen through the night. In the room, there was silence broken only by the boy's halting breaths.

Putting her nerves and trepidations aside, Barbara got down to work, monitoring and recording Stephen's heart rate and respirations and measuring his fluid input and output. She stood up the whole time. There was only one chair in the room, and a nursing student was asleep in it.

When she had arrived, Stephen was asleep, but a little later she heard the bell-like voice of a healthy child asking where he was, saying he felt fine, and asking if he could watch television.

Barbara was stunned and amazed that this critically injured boy could suddenly sound so normal. "Maybe tomorrow," she told him about the television set. "I don't think we have one right now. I'll see about finding one." [40]_Shortly afterward, Stephen went back to sleep.

Throughout the night, Stephen continued to wake, and speak to the nurse, just as if he were fine and in his own bed at home. Then he would doze off again.

Her long shift soon began drawing to a close and Barbara saw the sky outside the window brightening with the dawn. She looked down at her patient as his slow and steady breaths continued. At 7 a.m., a doctor reappeared. Then another, and another. Administrators, nurses, and students filed in and soon the room was once again crowded with people, just as it had been when Stephen was first brought in. Another nurse came in to relieve Barbara. She felt optimistic as she left. Stephen seemed more alert to her now. She knew from experience that once a critically ill patient survived the first night, the chances for recovery were good. She left the hospital in good spirits. It was going to be a beautiful, clear winter day.

The whole world soon learned of the survival of the little boy from Chicago. Methodist hospital received several hundred telephone calls and telegrams from all parts of the United States expressing hope for the youngster's recovery. Hundreds more had offered their blood and about 50 volunteered as skin donors in the battle to save Stephen.

The morning of December 17 saw Stevie progress and regress—alert, aware, and talking one minute, and lapsing into unconsciousness the next. He had asked his father whether he could have a book to read or watch television. Mr. Baltz promised to give him a portable television set for Christmas. Then the boy lapsed into unconsciousness.

He died at 1 p.m. Saturday, Dec 17.

Mrs. Baltz collapsed when she was informed of her son's death. She received sedatives and was put to bed in her room.

Barbara Scull learned of Stevie's death from the radio when she woke up that afternoon. The announcer said the death toll from the crash had gone up by one.

William Baltz gave the news of his son's death at 1:40 pm at a hastily gathered press conference in the ground-floor office of Rev. Stacey, the hospital's field chaplain. The chaplain invited reporters into the office and told them: "We have a very sad announcement for you. Mr. Baltz has been very courageous and has decided to tell you himself." [41]

Wringing his hands, his eyes clouded with tears, and his voice breaking, William Baltz addressed the gathered reporters and hospital staff: "Well, our Stevie passed away at 1 pm His mother and I are tremendously saddened. But we have had so many fine people in the world send sympathy and prayers, and we want to thank them. Stevie tried hard. Tried awfully hard. He was a wonderful boy, not because he was my son, but because he was Stevie. His mother and I thought Stevie would have been a tremendous and outstanding man. But we were not privileged to see him grow into manhood." He expressed thanks to the hospital staff and to the police for their efforts in behalf of his son. Making an effort to continue standing erect, he continued in a choking voice, "We have another son, William, Jr., who will be five in March, and a daughter, Randee, who will be ten on December 22. My very wonderful wife and I will make our home for Willie and little Randee." [42] "Stevie was a real fellow," Baltz said, before finally leaving the room.

After he was gone, the chaplain read the medical summary that had been handed him. "The chest injury," the chaplain read, "was so severe, resulting from the lungs being burned from the inhalation of flame, that it could not be combated or overcome. In spite of fluid therapy, cardiopulmonary support with tracheotomy and modern pacemaker support, all could not bring the little boy back from the effects of the severe injury." And he added his own footnote of the agony felt by everyone---"This is a devil of the thing," the chaplain said. "When you do everything—everything—and you lose out. God!" [43]

Back in Illinois, Pearl LeBlue, the Baltz family's nanny, heard the news of Stephen's death from neighbors as she was out walking with little Willie. She immediately took him to her home in Evanston, to spare him the knowledge of the tragedy. "I would rather his parents break it to him," she said. "I'm not letting him look at television either, because he might see a picture of Stephen or hear something about it and start asking questions." [44]

Sixty-five cents in change—five nickels and four dimes-- was found in Stephen Baltz's pockets. His father asked that it be put in the hospital chaplain's poor box. The coins were later made into a plaque which adorned a hospital wall as a permanent remembrance of the brave little boy who, if only for a short time, brought hope and optimism to a city shattered by grief.

10

Late Friday morning on the day of the crash, Christmas music played softly overhead at the arrival gates at both Idlewild and LaGuardia Airports as loved ones awaited the arrival of United 826 and TWA 266.

At Idlewild, families and friends watched at first with disappointment and then with nervous anxiety as United Airlines personnel continued to change the aircraft's expected arrival time on the flight board. When an agent finally removed the flight's listing from the board, panic set in for those gathered in the terminal. A United Airlines employee—a young red-haired woman--holding back tears, announced that United 826 would not arrive—it had crashed. Cries and screams erupted in the room. A woman began wailing, "What am I going to do? What am I going to do?" Ruth Sokolosky's husband Alvin was on the United flight and was returning home from a business trip to Colorado Springs, Colorado. The couple had just married November 20th. [45]

Fourteen families clustered tightly together in United's "Mariner's Room" on the airport's second floor, mingling and providing comfort to each other. A few slumped in chairs, their hands over their faces to hide tears.

George Loughran hoped that his son, Thomas, a Chicago representative of Standard and Poor, had changed his mind and taken another flight. Similarly, Richard Gordon hoped his 18-year-old daughter Susan had missed the flight. She was the student at the University of Wisconsin who had cheerfully signed off campus "Suzy Gordon—destination: New York---Home!! Woopee!"

Milton LaRiviere of Greenwich, CT, was waiting for his daughter Peggy. Then he was told she was dead. Peggy was a student at Barat College in Lake Forest, Illinois. Milton, a regional manager for General Electric had also just flown in that morning from a business trip in Chicago. He and Peggy had had planned to take the same flight but she was unable to get a seat on his plane.

In the midst of the potted plants and modern décor of the "Mariner's Room" Mr. and Mrs. Charles Dileo, were sitting with their daughter, Marjorie and sons Raymond and Ronnie, when they were told that their son, Frank, 21, had been killed. Mrs. Dileo collapsed as her husband and children tried to comfort her. They said they had particularly looked forward to Frank's Christmas holiday visit. A senior majoring in physical education at the University of Utah in Salt Lake City, this was to have been the first time in three years Frank had been home.

Some families waited at Idlewild for as much as six hours until all hope was gone that some passengers had missed the plane or changed their minds.

Many other family members waited anxiously in their homes as they watched the news unfolding on television and waited for the phone call they dreaded most. TWA flight attendant Margaret Gernat's family in Granville, New York had not heard anything about the plane crash in New York City. Though they would have gotten word via a phone call from the airline, the Gernats had no phone in their home. So, the heartbreaking task went to their neighbor, Mrs. Bruce Hammond. The TWA official who contacted her told her there was no final report on the dead, but there was unfortunately little hope that the flight attendant had survived. Her family had not seen Margaret for a few weeks, but they had received a letter from her saying she would be home for Christmas. Upon hearing the terrible news, the Gernats did what any parent would do, and as too many other family members across the country did, they broke down in tears.

The grim task remained of identifying the dead. The forty-four victims of the TWA crash had been taken from Staten Island's Seaview Hospital to Bellevue in the Kips Bay neighborhood of Manhattan. Until earlier in the year, Bellevue had been home to the New York City Medical Examiner Dr Milton Halpern's office on the second floor of the hospital. And though the ME moved out into a new building on First Avenue, he still maintained close contact with Bellevue.

Fourteen stone steps lead to the city mortuary in Bellevue Hospital. In the early morning hours and throughout the afternoon of December 17, friends and relatives of those who died in the TWA crash climbed those stairs. Most would not be going to the basement to view the remains of their loved ones. Officials discouraged them from doing that; other identification methods were available and more reliable given the state of most of the remains. They would be helpful, however, in providing valuable information to Detective John Aievoli, who for twenty-five years had headed the hospital's Bureau of Unidentified Dead. Dozens of detectives were at work in the high-ceilinged office and they spoke gently to the visitors—and even among themselves—as they worked at the piles of forms and documents, checking and double-checking the identifications they had made. Aievoli darted back and forth between his office and those where FBI identification experts compared the fingerprints of the dead with those in their files.

Next to the office where the detectives were hard at work, was a room, gray paint scaling on the walls, furnished with thirteen chairs and two wooden-backed sofas. Three fifteen-foot windows faced north across Twenty-ninth Street and other hospital buildings. The friends and family members of the TWA passengers waited there. Carter B. Helton Jr., whose father died in the crash, had traveled all night by train from his home in Dayton, Ohio. A dozen representatives of the airline, headed by John N. Martin, vice president in charge of sales, walked back and forth, doing whatever they could to be helpful.

Theodore Israel, 50, a New York businessman, made the first identification of a victim from the TWA airliner. It was his wife, Esta, who had been on a business trip to Columbus, Ohio.

The two bodies most mutilated in the TWA crash were identified with surprising ease at Bellevue. One was named because the wrist carried in death what must have been a cherished possession in life—a watch presented after 25 years of service with an insurance company. The other was identified by fingerprints.

Mary Burten of Jackson Heights had made her way to the temporary morgue set up in Staten Island for victims of the TWA crash. She wanted to see her husband, Arthur, one more time. The Burtens had a two-year-old daughter. Arthur had gone to Columbus on a business trip for Astron Corp. and had boarded the plane with his friend and colleague John Fisher who died with him in the crash. Mary was gently turned away from the Staten Island location and told to go to Bellevue, where all the TWA victims had been transferred.

William B. Horsey came from Massachusetts to identify the body of his brother, James who had briefly survived the TWA crash but perished on the way to the hospital.

Mrs. Ralph Fernandez and Miss Milagros Maldonado came to see Juanita Mullins. Juanita had been travelling from Dayton with her husband Cecil and their 3-month-old daughter to spend a Christmas holiday with their old friends in New York before going on to see Juanita's parents in Puerto Rico. Seven cousins, aunts, and uncles of Juanita Mullins had made the trek to the Bellevue Hospital morgue.

By 7:30 p.m. more than half the bodies at Bellevue—26—had been identified.

The dead from the United Airlines plane, and those who were killed on the Brooklyn streets, were brought to Kings County Hospital morgue located in the East Flatbush section of Brooklyn. At that hospital, family members were not permitted to attempt to visually identify their loved ones, even when they insisted. They were reassured that through dental charts, fingerprint records, medical histories, as well as personal effects that had survived the fires, a positive identification could be made without subjecting the families to the trauma of a difficult viewing. Where it was necessary for relatives or friends of a victim to identify the body directly, they were taken into a buff-colored seven by nine foot room with a four-seater bench, where a curtained window offered a view into another room. A body was brought into the room on a wheeled autopsy table and the curtain was drawn.

A distraught man forced his way past guards, determined to look for his friend, Charles Cooper—a street cleaner crushed on the streets of Brooklyn by the falling jet plane.

The identification process was long and time-consuming. By mid-afternoon on Saturday, only seven positive identifications had been made. There were 77 passengers of the United jet, including an infant, and seven crew members. In 90 morgue compartments had been assembled 81 bodies and parts and torsos of 9 others. By 7:30 pm, under the direction of Assistant Medical Examiner Dominick DiMaio, twenty tentative and fourteen positive identifications had been made.

11

Saturday, December 17th dawned windy and cold in New York City but the sun fought to shine through.

A scene that the day before was partially obscured by flames and smoke, now stood stark and nakedly clear. The corner of Sterling Place and Seventh Avenue looked like many European cities during WWII after an enemy air raid.

Working in shifts, hundreds of firemen dressed in black rubber coats with yellow stripes, hip boots, and helmets toiled tirelessly, as they raked through building rubble and cold ashes, and picked through piles of charred, crumbled metal for bodies. They were prepared to continue their search, day and night, without end until they were satisfied that every missing person was accounted for, every body was recovered, and every building was either safe for occupancy, or declared uninhabitable.   At 7:15 pm Friday, sixty-foot crane had begun to demolish the walls of brownstones condemned as unsafe, to permit firemen to seek other victims. The demolition was continued through the night.

The huge tail of the United Airlines DC-8, still intact, blocked the intersection of Sterling and 7th and still rested on the hood of Roy Rothenberg's red rental truck which bore the lettering of the Belfort Truck Renting Company. The truck, incredibly, given the devastation around it, was undamaged except for a cracked windshield.

The rest of the airplane was a jumble of scrap metal which lay strewn over 150 feet on Sterling Place. The nacelles of the jet engines and bits of the plane's wings were recognizable in the wreckage, but most of the debris was no more than scrap metal and ashes. The remains of incinerated automobiles lined the street.

In the afternoon, a yellow Sanitation Department snowplow dragged the biggest piece of the plane, a piece of a wing showing only the blue letters NITE (from the word UNITED), clear of the mass.

Nothing but rubble remained of the Pillar of Fire Church, with the exception of the stone Gothic portal bearing the church's now most ironic name.

The tenements on the northwest and southwest corners of Sterling Place and Seventh Avenue, while still standing, were gutted. Curtains streamed in the wind from blown out windows. Gaping holes showed nothing but sunlight and sky on the top floors of the buildings. Through the burned out holes in the tenements, onlookers could see an unfinished cup of coffee still sitting, untouched, on a charred table. Here and there could be seen a closet door still open where an occupant had stopped briefly to grab a coat on the way out. Nothing but charred cloth remained of the clothing left behind. In many of the apartments were the remains of gaily wrapped Christmas gifts—even some burned-out Christmas trees. An automobile, blasted off the street, was found in the cellar of McCaddin's funeral home.

On the intersection's southwest corner at 26 7th Avenue, the shop window of Jimmy's Chinese Laundry was gone, but the packaged laundry remained neatly stacked on the shelves and the lights were still burning. The grocery on the basement floor of the building suffered destruction of its outer wall and show window, but, oddly, the stocks of soda pop, canned goods, fresh fruits, and vegetables inside were undisturbed.

William Layer and other firemen spent Friday night and all day Saturday and Sunday searching the ruins of the building containing the butcher shop of Layer's father, Albert. They found one body, but William said it wasn't that of his father. They assumed Layer's father had run to the street and was mixed in with those unidentified bodies in the wreckage of the plane. According to one report, however, the body of the butcher, Albert Layer, was eventually found in the meat locker of his shop. It was surmised that Albert had gone into the meat locker either to retrieve a side of meat, or to escape the blast that shook the street outside his shop. The blast from the crash slammed the meat locker door shut, and Layer either suffocated inside or was roasted to death in his own freezer.

Many Park Slope residents had been forced to abandon their damaged homes and move in with relatives or into hotel rooms. Two brothers, Miles and Joseph Libhart, both artists, had to leave their apartment on Seventh Avenue and move into a hotel room which incurred for them a cost they could ill afford. When the brothers were eventually able to return to their apartment, they found it cold and dark. The winter's ice and cold had formed around everything, acting like a glue that stuck pictures fast to the walls, saucers to their cups, and books to their shelves. They picked through drawers and closets, only a candle for light, trying to salvage what they could of their art supplies, important papers, and other valuables. In the store below their apartment, Louis Czike, a candy salesman, had come back to his shop to find $260.00 worth of chocolate stolen from his store. Police officers had to be assigned to patrol the area of the burnt out and abandoned buildings to help prevent further loss by theft. [46]

It was the week before Christmas and businesses had been looking forward to the increase in shoppers to put them in the black. More than just the money, the proprietors enjoyed the spirit of the season, helping their customers—many of whom they personally knew from the neighborhood—to find that special gift, or just the right ingredients for their holiday meals. Many would have children returning home from college, or special friends visiting, which made the season all the more special. Now as they surveyed their shops for any damage, even the lucky ones whose businesses had escaped the devastation of the crash of the United airlines plane on the city street, were crestfallen at the fate of their neighbors and their own shops and businesses.

Joseph DiFrulo's Boy Scout troop 47 held a troop meeting. They were going to help out at the crash scene by bringing donuts and coffee to the firemen and the policemen. When they got there, being kids, the first thing they looked for were bodies, but they had already been removed. What they did see was burnt jet fuel, pitch black and plenty of it. The smell was so acrid, Joseph decided he didn't want to be there anymore, so he said to a friend, "I think we need to leave because it's really getting to me." The two boys wandered away from their troop and walked by the bowling alley, which had been turned into a temporary morgue for the victims of the crash. There they saw bodies but they were already covered up. The bodies were lined up in the alleys. It seemed so bizarre to him. He and his friend were enlisted to bring coffee to the people working there and that's how they spent the rest of their time at the scene.

Harry Mangieri sat glumly in his quiet Plaza Bowling Center at 11 Seventh Avenue. His center had been used as a temporary morgue, and a gathering place for rescuers to keep warm and get a cup of coffee offered by the Salvation Army and Red Cross volunteers. Now, the next day, his sixteen alleys lay dark and unused. Firemen, policemen, Civil Defense men, sanitation workers and others on the job still used the place to get warm and rest, but no one would be coming in to bowl. No birthday or holiday parties would be booked in his establishment. Mr. Mangieri estimated he would lose $2000 in business this weekend.

A candy store, toy store, drug store, liquor store, and other shops near the busy corner of Flatbush and Seventh Avenues, which were not damaged but which were behind police barriers, were suffering heavy losses on this last shopping weekend before Christmas.

"Kindly keep moving, please," patrolmen called through loudspeakers to throngs of sightseers who shuffled curiously along the barriers in Flatbush Avenue. "Don't block the crosswalk."

Night fell, and two dozen powerful searchlights lit up the scene of horror in Brooklyn as the rescue workers continued to dig into the rubble.

City agencies worked tirelessly to find housing for people whose apartments were destroyed in the crash. The Welfare Department found temporary housing for twenty-two families and individuals, including eight families on its public assistance rolls. William Reid, chairman of the city housing authority, and his agency did all it could to place the homeless families in vacant apartments in New York City housing authority projects.

There was a mail problem for survivors unable to return to their apartments. How would they now get their Christmas packages and cards? The Post Office set up a truck a block away at Flatbush Avenue as a mobile Post Office. The displaced called there for undelivered mail. Nearly 3,000 pounds of mail coming from Chicago consisting of more than 129,000 letters was aboard the United Air Lines plane and was feared to be strewn over the streets after the crash. Postal inspectors set out to examine every scrap of paper in the rubble searching for the mail.

On Staten Island, and in the Park Slope neighborhood of Brooklyn, business owners, residents, public servants, and government and volunteer agencies worked through a growing sense of despair, grief, and exhaustion to accomplish the Herculean task of restoring the neighbors and the city itself to some sense of normalcy. Christmas was but one week away. Everyone was determined it would be a happy and joyous one—filled with family, friends, and comradery. But perhaps most of all, a deeper appreciation of the fragility of life—and find within it the very preciousness of that life to all of them.

In the days and weeks following the tragic collision of the United and TWA planes over New York, dozens of funerals, requiems, and memorial services were held for the victims not just in the Chicago area and New York, but all across the country; one service even taking place in Nice, France, the final resting place for Mrs. Edwige Dumalski and her two children Joelle, 12 and Patrick 14.

Barat College in Lake Forest, Illinois scheduled a memorial service for sophomore Ann Hodgins and freshman Peggy LaRiviere for January 5th, after all the college's students would have returned from their Christmas break.

United flight attendant, twenty-three-year-old Mary Mahoney, was remembered at a funeral mass on December 22 in St. Clare de Monte Falco church in Chicago. The plane's Flight Engineer, Richard Prewitt, was memorialized at the Keystone Baptist Church in Torrance, California on December 19. The mass was followed by another funeral service in Taylor, California—the home of Prewitt's mother and brother.

Young Stephen Baltz made his final flight aboard a United Air Lines jet as his body was flown from New York to his home in Chicago. His family returned by train.

Two young Gridley, California boys--Stephen and Jim Brady were deeply affected by the story of Stephen and his brave fight to survive the days after the crash. Saddened for his family, the two boys sat down and wrote a letter to the Baltz family. Not knowing where they lived and how to get the letter to them, the boys, on the suggestion of their father who was a policeman, posted the letter to the Chicago Police Department knowing they would get it to the family.

The letter, addressed "Dear Chief of Police," read: "We want to tell you how sorry we are about your little boy Steven, but we no [sic] he will have a nice Christmas in heaven with Jesus. We prayed for him…We are sending you some money to get Steven some flowers with. My dad is a policeman and we get 50 cents a week so we are sending it to you for the flowers. We got our money for next week too, so we got $2 to send. Will you let us know if you get our letter? We hope you have a nice Christmas. We hope we get a fishen [sic] pole or a B-B gun. Send our letter to us at 864 Indiana St., Gridley, California." [47]

On December 20, Stephen Baltz was buried in Skokie, Illinois as a cold wind swirled snow around his gravesite. A giant, snow laden pine tree towered over the grave. The family and the fifty friends and relatives who also attended the ceremony, were sheltered from the snow under a canopy.

The funeral services, held immediately before the burial, drew 300 persons to the chapel of the First Methodist Church of Evanston, where Stephen had been baptized in February of 1949. "Birth and death are essential parts of God's life," said the pastor, Dr. Harold A. Bosely, in the services there. "Each one is surrounded by mystery we cannot penetrate, but God's goodness continues through death." He told the mourners that the true measure of life is not to be found in the number of years, but in quality. "Love and loss go hand in hand," he said. "If there is no love, there is no loss. The presence of love is what makes loss so hard." [48]

12

The largest number of Civil Aeronautics Board (CAB) experts ever assembled for such a task took on the investigation of the December 16th crash of United 826 and TWA 266. More than one hundred Federal agents were sent to study wreckage, examine tapes of conversations between control towers and the planes, and question control tower personnel. The CAB sent board members G. Joseph Minetti and Alan S. Boyd, and 31 investigators from Washington. Melvin N. Gough, Director of the Bureau of Safety, was to head the investigating team. Joseph Fluet, chief of the Operations Division of the Bureau of Safety and former supervisor of the bureau in the New York region, also flew to New York. The Federal Aviation Administration (FAA), responsible for control of the airways, and under the direction of E. R. Quesada, also sent its own investigators. Investigation headquarters were set up at the Seaway Idlewild Hotel, near the Federal Building at Idlewild, where the CAB and FAA had their regional offices.

The flight data recorder (FDR) from the United jet was recovered in the rubble of the Pillar of Fire Church. Blackened and dented, the 8-by-8-by-16-inch device was removed to International Airport where technicians carefully removed the steel tape containing information on the plane's speed, altitude, direction, and time. The data gleaned from the device would be compared with radio communications and radar information in hopes that it would hold the secret of what caused the disaster. At the time of the accident, the recording device was required by law to be on all planes which flew above 25,000 feet, as do jets so the TWA plane carried no flight recorder. Flight data recorders were first introduced in the 1950s but it was not until 1965 that FDRs (commonly called "black boxes") were painted bright orange or yellow to make them easier to locate at crash sites.

Agents examining the first part of the recorder's tape found it undamaged. The tape, without being further uncoiled, was then sent to CAB headquarters in Washington for relay to the recorder's manufacturer in California.

The remains of both planes were shipped to LaGuardia Airport for study. Investigators worked all the first night sifting through the plane wreckage, then met in the morning at Idlewild International Airport to compare notes.

Before the investigation was barely underway, FAA Administrator Quesada told reporters that it was "very probable" there had been a collision between the two planes.[49] The CAB was not as anxious to jump to a conclusion so quickly. CAB member Alan S. Boyd was present when Quesada made his statement at the airport. The two officials held a joint news conference. They said that the investigation was just starting and little had been learned, but that they knew the TWA plane had fallen in three parts in Staten Island in a way indicating that it could not have been broken up by hitting the ground. This made it appear likely there had been a collision, but there was as yet no positive evidence. "All we know is that two planes crashed eleven miles apart," they said.[50]

Civil Aeronautics Board member Minetti announced at the news conference that the investigators were concentrating on five phases of the crash. His investigators were split into teams to examine each of the five phases: operations, aircraft structure, human factors, power plants, and weather.

Three days after the crash, FAA Chief Quesada, briefed president Eisenhower. Once again jumping the gun in the investigation, he told newsmen that the pilot of the DC-8 failed to follow instructions to stay in his assigned holding pattern. Quesada also said that it was a "known fact" that one of two electronic navigational systems aboard the jet was "nonfunctional and out of commission" at the time of the collision.

In addition to positing early on that the United Air Lines plane had strayed outside of its given instructions for some yet to be determined reason, Quesada defended the agency's radar surveillance procedures saying that Idlewild airport's approach control was "prepared and ready" to guide the United DC-8 jet into Idlewild but could not locate the plane in or near the pattern to which it had been assigned. The radio signals that locate the Preston aircraft holding pattern over the New Jersey shore were operating normally when two airliners collided as confirmed by flight checks with specialized FAA craft carrying calibrated electronic equipment, he said.

Representatives from the airline, however, were not so quick to take on this theory of United Air Line pilot error and struck back at Quesada for drawing such a quick conclusion. W.A. Patterson, President of United Air Lines, challenged an account of the disaster given by Quesada in which he said that the United jet was flying an unauthorized course. "Yesterday, the administrator of the FAA made certain statements to the press that, regardless of his intent, leave the impression this morning that this flight was carelessly operated and that there was a disregard of instructions from the FAA. We cannot permit such an impression to exist. If the administrator is capable of issuing statements of this kind, then, I assume, as administrator of the FAA, he can also talk with authority about the affairs of that agency." [51]

In his reply to United, Quesada declared he had never said the United plane was carelessly operated; he had adhered to simple and "obvious" facts about the collision, namely, that the jet had proceeded beyond the Preston holding pattern as evidenced by the fact that the collision occurred in the vicinity of Miller Field on Staten Island, a point approximately eleven miles away from Preston.

For their part, the airline questioned why the Air Traffic Controllers had not picked up the United plane on radar after it passed the Preston intersection, when they would have had the obvious opportunity to avert the disaster. On radar surveillance Quesada said the area traffic control center had discontinued radar coverage of the United jet as it approached Preston in accordance with "standard procedures." He contended that there was no "prescribed" requirement for the Idlewild control tower to pick up radar surveillance immediately from the area center. Radar service is not provided to planes in a holding pattern, he said, due to a problem of identifying constantly merging targets.

Criticism of the FAA came from another corner. Clarence N. Sayen, president of the Air Line Pilots Association, who in the past had publicly traded words with the FAA Chief on several pilot-safety problems, accused Quesada of "irresponsible abuse of public office" for premature statements he made on the collision, saying that "to issue statements at this time which even infer [sic] that certain events led to this accident is sheer speculation." [52] Sayen, who was President of the Air Line Pilots' Association for 11 years, was later to die in a plane crash himself when the United 727 jet in which he was a passenger plunged into Lake Michigan on a flight from New York's LaGuardia Airport to Chicago O'Hare in August 1965.

On New Year's Day 1961, Quesada appeared on NBC's TV news program Meet the Press. On the program, Quesada implied that the airliner collision might have been averted if one of the pilots had called for help from the ground. To illuminate his point, he told the moderator, Ned Brooks, that just before the collision, a Pan American airliner had asked air traffic controllers for help after they suffered a partial failure of their navigational equipment. The failure, Quesada pointed out, was similar to that experienced by the United jet, whose pilots chose not only not to request ATC assistance, but failed to even report the problem to ground controllers. In the case of the Pan Am airliner, ATC assisted them to a safe landing at New York International Airport. Such assistance was extended frequently and successfully to pilots who ask for it, Quesada said. But ultimately, he offered, "navigation lies in the hands of the pilot." When Brooks asked whether he was saying the Dec 16 disaster was due to pilot error, Quesada replied, "I'm not saying that, you are….You can interpret that any way you wish." [53]

Quesada's past conflicts with the Airline Pilots' Association were well known and documented at this time. Addressing these conflicts, Brooks asked Quesada if he felt the pilots' association and airplane owners were standing in the way of proper air safety regulations. "That's not too erroneous," he said. Quesada explained that the pilots and owner groups have resisted some FAA regulations. But, he said in reply to another question, this has had no serious effect on the safety of air passengers because his agency always overcomes the resistance.

Discussion of the accident in the press generated considerable acrimony. On January 3, just prior to the opening of the CAB hearings into the disaster, Francis M. McDermott, executive director of the Air Traffic Control Association representing 9,500 controller, pilot, and industry members, told the press that control of air traffic was in a "more precarious" state today than it was three years before-- before the Government stepped up efforts to relieve the hazards. Openly criticizing the working conditions and pay scales of controllers, he charged that superior personnel were "discouraged from embarking upon such a hazardous and unrewarding occupation." At a news conference later, he said: "There is a distinct feeling among experienced controllers that the new people simply don't measure up to the requirements of this job." [54]

McDermott, charged that "time had almost run out on our antiquated system" of jet-age air traffic control. He asserted that if the air traffic control system problems had been attacked vigorously after the 1956 Grand Canyon crash, also between United and TWA planes, the New York collision might have been averted. Failure to heed this second warning, he said, will put "the lives of hundreds of thousands of airline passengers and the future of the aviation industry" in "serious jeopardy."[55] McDermott said Congress should "seek an accounting" on a year-late study on strengthening the present air traffic control service. There was no doubt that McDermott's comments were directed, at least in part, at the FAA director. Quesada had just resigned his post on January 3rd to take over ownership of the new Washington Senators baseball expansion franchise.

    The CAB opened its public inquiry in the crowded main ballroom of the Hotel St. George in Brooklyn on January 4, 1961. Over 125 witnesses would be called and questioned not only by the fifteen CAB investigators who probed the crash, but by some thirty representatives of ten interested parties including both airlines, the FAA, the Air Line Pilots' Association, Douglas and Lockheed corporations, Airlines Stewards' and Stewardess' Association, Flight Engineers Association, Airlines Dispatchers Association, and Air Traffic Control Association.

    On the first day of testimony, civilian witnesses appeared before the panel to give their account of what they saw. Among the witnesses were six who saw the TWA plane as it fell over Staten Island, where the TWA plane crashed including the florist, Paul Kleinau, and four who witnessed the jet crash in Brooklyn including Brother Conrad Barnes who testified to seeing the United jet heading straight toward St Augustine's school where he watched in horror with his students. In testimony by the eyewitnesses, although seven testified to seeing the planes just before the collision, it was evident that only a few actually saw the collision itself; most saw only pieces of the planes falling. Reconstruction of the wreckage had previously indicated that either the jet had attempted to gain last-minute altitude or the Connie had tried, vainly, to dive for safety but George R. Baker, CAB air safety investigator, reported that no one noticed any evasive maneuvering by either plane as they converged on their low-level collision course over Staten Island.

    Joseph Zamuda, chairman of the flight operations group in CAB's Bureau of Air Safety reported that all navigational facilities serving International Airport and LaGuardia field, where the doomed planes were headed, seemed to have been operating normally—except for "course sensitivity" at the Colt's Neck, NJ omni-range station. Colt's Neck was one of several omni-range stations where the pilot of the United Air Lines DC-8 jet might have tuned in for a bearing. Observers said that if the "course sensitivity" was faulty, he might have gone slightly off course. However, there was no evidence that he even used Colt's Neck and Zamuda drew no conclusions.

Alan Brunstein, CAB Meteorologist, reported on the weather conditions present on the day of the crash. He noted that practically all pilots reported that from 1,500 feet to 10,000 feet, they were on solid instruments.

CAB investigator, David Thompson, in his review of the conversation between the DC-8 and air traffic controllers on the ground testified as to his doubt about the reported transmission from the United jet's pilot of "We'll dump it." The pilot was reported saying this in regard to his desire to stay above the weather until he needed to come quickly down into the holding pattern at Preston. The phrase was sometimes used by pilots to indicate that they will descend rapidly from a given altitude to a lower one, but in this case, Thompson asserted that he did not believe this was what the pilot said. He said the radio call from the DC-8 at this point began with an unintelligible first word; was followed by "...er, will head it right on down..." and this was followed by another word that could not be understood. The tape with these transcribed words on it had been turned over to the Bell Telephone Laboratories for speech analysis, Thompson said, in hopes that the laboratory could determine what the garbled words were. This call from the DC-8 was made at a critical point in the flight-- about three minutes before the final message was received from the jet, indicating the plane was approaching the Preston holding pattern over New Jersey at 5,000 feet.

Experts pinpointed the exact crash site as well as the approximate time of the crash. Although witnesses put the time at 10:30 to 10:35 am, the six-second unintelligible, open-mike transmission from the TWA plane was recorded on the ground at 10:33:44. This seemed about as close, in seconds, as could be reconstructed as to the actual time of the collision. Recorded conversations with the United DC-8 bore out the approximate time. At 10:33:28 am, the DC-8 notified International approach control that it was "approaching Preston at 5,000." Preston was where the jet was to remain until brought in for landing but apparently, it was then already over Staten Island and only some 14 to 15 seconds from disaster. There was no further word from the jet.

On the second day of the inquiry, a strong effort was made to place at least part of the blame for the airliner collision on lapses and inadequacies in air traffic control procedures. Federal officials in charge of traffic control were bombarded with questions by CAB representatives, United Air Lines, the pilot's union and other groups. The main focus of their questioning was why, when the United DC-8 jet flew past the area where it was supposed to circle, radar controllers had not detected the fact and radioed a warning to the pilot.

The burden of answering these pointed questions fell to the FAA, as the agency responsible for air traffic control. FAA officials responded that the traffic system does not have the capability of affording a constant radar watch to every plane in its control, and therefore controllers are not required to maintain such a watch, although they are supposed to offer as much surveillance as they can. To function safely, the system required that pilots follow the traffic instructions given them.

Roys Jones, FAA's program planning board chief, testified that the New York Center turned over the jet to International approach control at 10:33:16 am. He explained that when planes depart one controller's area of responsibility, there is a "radar handoff"—that is, the craft is seen on the radarscope of both the controllers handing off the aircraft and the scope at the receiving airport before the latter takes over responsibility for it. However, in this case, the United jet was not seen on the International scope at the change-over. Even so, Jones contended had the jet remained at Preston, as instructed, there could have been no collision.

Van R. O'Brien, a member of CAB's board of inquiry asked Jones: who was responsible for alerting a pilot if he went beyond his holding area?

"Whatever radar has him," Jones answered. However, when the plane was turned over to the approach control, there was no radar surveillance at that particular moment.

O'Brien pressed Jones to answer, "Who was responsible for the plane's position."

"Nobody," Jones replied.

"In a dense area like New York, shouldn't we have planes watched?" O'Brien asked.

"If we had the capabilities, yes," Jones said, "But 826 was told to hold (at Preston)." [56]

The highest ranking FAA witness on the second day of testimony was David D. Thomas, head of the Bureau of Air Traffic Management. The first to question Mr. Thomas was United's legal vice president, Charles F. McErlean who read from an FAA directive calling for radar controllers to follow jet traffic and to radio direction changes if their scopes showed any danger of a collision with another plane. McErlean asked, shouldn't United's DC-8 therefore have been given constant radar coverage all the way to its intended landing point at New York International Airport?

"No," Mr. Thomas replied. He explained that constant radar coverage was required only above 24,000 feet, where jets flew fastest and human eyesight was least reliable in avoiding collisions. He conceded that his agency would like to be able to offer continuous radar surveillance of flights.

"This is our objective," he said, "but it has not yet been met." But he insisted that the transfer from the New York Center to International, "was done under completely normal procedures." [57]

A similar thread was followed in questioning by Capt. J.D. Smith, regional safety chairman of the Air Line Pilots Association. The pilots' union was intent on insuring that the pilots who died in the accident did not come in for unjust blame. While officials generally accepted that the jet flew off course what was not known was why. Was it human error by an air crewman or a ground controller? Or could there have been a malfunction in navigation or other equipment aboard the plane or on the ground? Captain Smith spent considerable time trying to determine why—rules aside— there had been a gap in radar tracking. Why was it impossible, Captain Smith asked, to affect an unbroken hand-off of a plane from the area controller to the tower? He inquired of FAA's Roys Jones whether the transfer of the jet to International occurred "over Preston or in the vicinity of Preston," Jones answered: "At 10:33:16, New York Center turned over to International approach control. Prior to that, he had been cleared only to the fix (Preston) and given holding instructions. There was no reason to believe he was any place other than the holding fix." The transfer, from the New York Center to International, Jones asserted, "was done under completely normal procedures... The aircraft was cleared to the Preston intersection. As far as the system was concerned, there was no lack or loss of control."[58]

The third day of the hearings, investigators heard four pilots testify that they themselves had experienced difficulties with the Colt's Neck omnirange station signal on the same day the United jet collided with the TWA plane. The Colt's Neck station, located eight miles west of Long Branch, NJ and ten miles southeast of the Preston holding point to which the doomed United flight was directed, was one of three stations normally used to locate Preston. If it was malfunctioning at the time of the accident, it could have accounted for the jet straying off course.

Two of the captains who testified to difficulties with Colt's Neck were with United. The other two with American Airlines.

The most dramatic testimony came from United pilot Capt. William J. Picune, who was flying the same course as United 826. His passengers were company personnel coming to New York as a result of the disaster. Picune asserted that about 2:45 pm on December 16, only some four hours after the collision, while waiting to pick up the Colt's Neck beam, he found himself over water, five or six miles off Staten Island a few miles from Miller Field, where the remains of the TWA plane had landed. They could see the wreckage from their window. This was five or six miles beyond Preston—beyond the point where he should have picked up the Colt's Neck beam. "There was no mention of my being north of the Preston holding pattern by International approach control," he asserted.

"Are you under the impression that you are always under radar surveillance?" asked Capt. J.D. Smith, of the Airlines Pilots' Association.

"I was –up to this meeting—believe me!" Picune answered fervently.[59] Picune admitted that he did not report the incident to the FAA until December 28, because "I never gave it any thought."[60] Under questioning from FAA attorney William Crawford, Picune was forced to change his testimony, when presented a transcript of an Idlewild tower recording showing the pilot was advised by Idlewild that he was "wide" of Preston and had been ordered to make a sharp right turn to get back into the pattern, thus refuting his claim that he was never informed he was off course. [61]

United Capt. Paul Wallace testified that at 6:30 pm on the 16th he received "an erroneous signal" from Colt's Neck indicating that he was over Preston, but his instruments showed he had not yet arrived in that spot. Capt. Walter P. Moran, a veteran American Airlines pilot, said at about 3:30 pm he discovered "an area of nil radio reception" from Colt's Neck while he was on a training flight in a Boeing 707 from Detroit to Idlewild Airport. He told the panel that the reception was absent for a long enough time to necessitate his changing his flight plans. On another flight he piloted on

December 20, Moran said he encountered the same problem with the Colt's Neck signal. Another American Airlines pilot, William S. McCormick, testified he noticed a problem with the Colt's Neck station signal as he was taking off from Idlewild at about 9:33 am on December 16. He lost the signal for three or four minutes and a warning flag popped up on his instrument panel.[62] None of the four pilots reported their trouble with the beacon until the day after the collision, stating they did not realize the seriousness of the situation until after the crash.

Three additional witnesses testified they had no knowledge of any difficulties at the Colt's Neck station. One, Joseph T. Cincotta, an FAA inspector, testified that he was riding in the cockpit with Captain Wallace on December 16 and despite the fact that Wallace testified to having trouble with the signal, Cincotta observed nothing unusual. "If the captain had made some remark that he was having trouble I certainly would have heard it," he asserted.[63] Another pilot, Captain Richard J. Gosnell, of Capital Airlines, told the panel that he had used the Colt's Neck beacon without difficulty on the morning of the accident while flying to LaGuardia Airport. American Airlines pilot, Capt. S.N. Reed had reported being over Preston on the approach to International Airport at 10:40 am, seven minutes after the accident. The Colts Neck signal appeared normal at that time, he said.

The FAA held to their position that all their facilities were functioning properly on the day of the crash. After the hearing, Joseph D. Blatt, FAA New York region administrator, said warning signals would have sounded in monitoring stations if the signals were off more than one compass degree.[64] The pilots who had testified to having had no problem with the Colt's Neck signal had been flying closest to the time United 826 would have been in the vicinity. Unlike Captains Picune, Wallace, and McCormick, they had flown the same course, under the same Instrument Flight Rules conditions, and at the same altitude as United 826 and had noted no problem with the signal.

The fourth day of testimony began on Monday, January 9 with John F. Pahl, chief of the engineering division of the Civil Aeronautics Board, testifying about the readings obtained from the United jet's Flight Data Recorder (FDR). This marked the first time in the history of crash inquiries in the U. S. that precise data from a flight recorder had been introduced. Pahl testified that, according to the analysis of the FDR, the United DC-8 was traveling more than 500 miles an hour when it swept past its assigned circling point at the Preston holding area. This was 260 miles an hour faster than a plane was legally dictated to travel when circling in its holding pattern. In addition, the jet was at an altitude of 8,700 feet as it passed the circling point. This was 3,700 feet higher than the 5,000 foot level where the plane should have started circling while awaiting clearance to land at New York International Airport. Pahl also testified to the following facts: The jet was being pushed by a tail wind of about thirty-eight miles an hour as it passed the holding point; it was losing altitude at a rate of 3,600 feet a minute; the jet's speed had been reduced to 363 miles an hour when the collision occurred one mile west of Miller Army Air Field; and the plane's altitude at the time of the collision was between 5,250 and 5,175 feet. The reconstruction of the jet's flight path also showed a corner-cutting turn as it headed onto the final track that was to send it smashing into the right side of the TWA Super Constellation.

Charles F. McErlean, United Air Lines legal representative, said he had no quarrel with the flight recorder's account, but reiterated that United felt its pilot was not at fault. United also argued that though their jet had made a rapid, fairly steep descent, there was nothing abnormal or illegal about it. The pilot had been slowing down, in anticipation of reaching Preston, when the collision occurred. He was not required to be at legal holding speed until actually in the circling pattern. McErlean contended that the pilot never got into the pattern because he never got the proper signal from the ground station that he was passing Preston.

The fifth day of the CAB hearings heard testimony about the captain of the United plane, Robert Sawyer, and further defense by United representatives that their experienced pilot would not have strayed past his directed holding pattern had there not been some malfunction in the radar equipment under the jurisdiction of the FAA. Capt. I.E. "Gus" Sommermeyer, United vice-president in charge of flying, opined that Sawyer must have still thought himself south of the Preston holding area when he collided with the TWA plane. Sommermeyer persisted in the airline's stance that something was wrong with the Colt's Neck signal, as several pilots flying the same day of the crash had previously testified, and despite the FAA's assertions that testing of the station performed within hours of the crash indicated no problem with the signal. Additionally, Sommermeyer criticized the FAA for not providing continuous radar surveillance of commercial aircraft. "It is my belief in retrospect," Sommermeyer said, "that Capt. Sawyer fully expected radar direction from the time his clearance to Idlewild was revised at about the time he was passing over Allentown, PA. The revised clearance reduced the total distance of the flight and speeded up the flight's arrival by a minute or two, but the change in directions to be flown, the airways to be followed, and the intersections where turns were to be made undoubtedly demanded a hasty revision in the captain's mind of all the estimated times of arrival at these points that had been established by the original plan." Sommermeyer went on, "I am certain that, putting myself in Sawyer's position on Dec 16, I would not have had time to make new computations and I would have depended on outside assistance, mainly the radar, for making my fixes. The FAA representatives who have testified before this panel," Sommermeyer continued in his assault on the agency, "have stated that United Air Lines would not expect complete radar of its jets from take-off to landing. But this is not what the administrator has been saying." [65]

"I have in my pocket," he continued, "a speech which the administrator made before the National Press club in Washington as late as Nov 17, 1960, in which he said that without the application of a vast number of military radars to the civil air traffic control system of the country, full radar coverage of the jet from take-off to destination would not have been possible. This is what the FAA has been telling us," Sommermeyer said, "and this is the impression that I have had as a captain in scheduled service and I am sure that the majority of our pilots understood that this radar surveillance—all the way—has been given to the jet operations."[66]

Wednesday, January 11, the sixth day of hearings on the December 16th crash, FAA Administrator, Quesada announced that his agency planned to study the flight paths followed by about forty jetliner flights prior to the Dec 16 collision to see if pilots were engaging in dangerous practices and to determine if action was necessary to change flight rules or to enforce compliance with existing rules. Quesada indicated that the FAA might punish pilots or their airlines for rules violations that turned up in the study of earlier flights. Quesada had asked United for the flight recorder tapes of the last twenty United jets entering the New York air space before the crash.

The attorney for United, Charles F. McErlean, took the floor at the opening of the afternoon session to announce that his company had received the request from FAA Administrator Quesada for recorders from other United jets that had flown into New York.

"We understand," he said acidly, "that the CAB has the only jurisdiction to investigate this accident, its cause, and to make recommendations to avoid a repetition in the future."[67] He told the CAB panel that United would furnish the requested records not to the FAA, but to the CAB investigating board, and through that body, he said, if the FAA wanted to see the records, they could.

In another development, United introduced a report by an Eastern Air Lines pilot of a misalignment of a radio beam by which the United pilot might have been navigating. It said that the Eastern pilot, Capt. P.J. Slayden, had encountered the trouble the day before the collision and had told the FAA traffic-control center about it.

Wayne Hendershot, FAA chief of air traffic management announced that as a precaution, given the facts so far revealed about possible contributing factors to the disaster, jet liners were now being routed via the Robbinsville, NJ omnirange station in order to give pilots a better opportunity to realign their course before entering the holding pattern. Hendershot also testified that heavy approach traffic just before the accident apparently prevented continuous radar coverage of the United jet. The radar controller of the New York center, he said, was watching three other planes inbound from Preston---two for International Airport and one for LaGuardia. This preoccupation prevented a normal radar handoff, in which the center's controller would have notified International's approach control that the United jet was coming in.

"If the air traffic controller was not providing radar vectoring (guiding) to the plane, who was responsible for the plane's navigation?" a United representative asked.

"The pilot," said Hendershot. [68] He reminded the assembled body that the United plane had been cleared only to Preston and if it had entered the directed holding pattern there would have been no accident.

Day seven saw dramatic testimony from William L. Smith, the air traffic approach controller at LaGuardia Airport who was guiding the TWA Constellation into its landing pattern at the time of the crash. Smith recounted his experience of seeing the blip, which was later learned to have been United Flight 826, approaching the Constellation and the two warnings he gave Wollam, the TWA pilot.

He watched as the blips merged on the screen, then separated. Since air traffic control radar did not, at that time, show altitude, Smith could not have known when he saw the merging blips that they were both at 5,000 feet. Smith testified that he had no reason to expect another plane approaching at the 5,000 foot elevation without his knowledge. The TWA plane, he said, was coming in just as it should.

During questioning, Smith was asked, "Did you expect the pilot, after you advised him that another target was approaching, to ask for another vector?"

"I might have," Smith replied. [69]

Smith was asked why he didn't instruct Wollam to make a turn away from the approaching aircraft, since it was unknown if they were at the same altitude.

"Because the pilot had not requested a vector [change of course]," Smith replied. "I have been instructed not to give a pilot a vector around unidentified planes unless he requests it." [70]

Earlier, William A. Parenteau, chief controller at International Airport, for which the United jet was bound, testified the jet was not picked up on his tower screens before the crash. He was asked whether an approach controller would inform an identified plane it had strayed from its course or pattern if he observed this on radar.

"He would normally," Parenteau answered, "but there had been some criticism of this on the part of the pilots who have advised us they are flying the plane and we should only provide control and necessary separation from other aircraft." [71]

It was no secret that there was often a tense relationship between the FAA and airline pilots and their representatives. Pilots wanted independence to fly their planes, but at the same time, expected the FAA's air traffic control system to protect the airways and give guidance for flight paths and landing instructions.

The day's sessions ended early so the inquiry officials could visit the LaGuardia and International control towers.

On January 13th, a Friday, the CAB held the eighth and final day of official hearings on the investigation of the collision between United Air Lines Flight 826 and TWA Flight 266. The day was marked by a bitter attack by United Air Lines representatives on the state of the nation's air traffic control system.

Testimony was heard from a long list of traffic controllers who were on duty in three radar rooms at the time of the crash. Three who manned a critical control station were Ronald DiGiovanni, John D. Fischer, and Harold L. Brown.

DiGiovanni controlled the United jet as it flew southeast from Allentown, PA, turned up airway Victor 123, and headed for the Preston NJ intersection of two radio beams—the point where it had been instructed to start circling. He testified that he had last noted the jet's blip when the plane was from one to three miles southwest of Preston. The time was somewhere between 10:33:01 and 10:33:14.

Earlier evidence presented had set the time of the collision somewhere between 10:33:33 and 10:33:44. DiGiovanni's time estimates were contradictory to the facts, as the United jet could not have possibly travelled the 13-16 miles distance between the spot he stated he saw the plane near Preston and the point of the collision. William Crawford, attorney for the FAA, stressed that the agency's position was that the collision time had not been accurately fixed at the 10:33:33 to 10:33:44 time frame.

DiGiovanni, admitted that when he instructed the inbound United jet to enter the Preston holding pattern in New Jersey and terminated his control of it, he did not look at his radar screen. There was no allegation that DiGiovanni violated regulations by not looking, but if he had done so, he might have noticed that the DC-8 was overshooting the pattern and then have issued a warning.

Herbert Rausch, of the International Airport approach control center, whose task it was to direct the jet on from Preston, testified that at 10:33:28 am—eight seconds after DiGiovanni's signoff—the United pilot advised him he was "approaching Preston" at 5,000 feet. But both Rausch and his supervisor, Peter W. Bernhard, said they looked and could not find the jet on their screen. Actually, the jet was beyond Preston and nearing collision over Staten Island.

In a prepared statement to the Board of inquiry, United attorney Charles McErlean charged that the collision would never have happened have the air traffic control system been making full use of its available facilities and personnel and urged Congress to take action to prevent a recurrence of such a tragedy in the future.

In his statement, McErlean said: "Frankly, we have been shocked at some of the things we have learned since this investigation started. These facts should be of extreme interest and concern to the carriers who are parties, as well as the other parties to this investigation. In addition, we believe that these matters are, or ought to be, of extreme concern to all the other air transport carriers of this country, other users of the system, and all those interested in aviation today. In this we include not only private organizations and individuals, but also agencies of the government and the Congress of the United States. In our opinion, no air line or other aviation interest in the country can ignore the record that has been made here nor can the Congress. We must now take the necessary steps to establish and maintain...a system that provides the degree of safety that will prevent any recurrence of the tragedy of Dec 16...If we do otherwise, we will be living in a fool's paradise." [72]

William Crawford, attorney for the FAA, countered McErlean's charges by stating that such charges contributed nothing to the Board's efforts to determine the probable cause of the accident. Criticisms of the air traffic control system notwithstanding, the essential element of the accident could not be overlooked and that is that the pilot of the United jet, for some reason, committed a cardinal sin under air traffic rules by traveling 10 to 12 miles beyond the last radio navigational fix to which it had been cleared.

From the evidence presented in the eight days of hearings, Crawford, McErlean, and J.D. Smith of the Pilots' Association all agreed it was impossible to determine what had caused the collision. Further tests and analysis would be needed, and various laboratories around the country would be conducting such tests to aid in the investigation.

Three main points had been established and agreed upon by all parties to the hearings:

1. The jet was off course
2. It was traveling more than 500 miles an hour when it was over its assigned circling point at Preston but slowed rapidly and could easily have stayed within the bounds of the Preston holding area
3. Radar controllers did not continuously watch the jet's radar blip.

CAB Chairman G. Joseph Minetti announced that the board would study the facts presented, and invited communications in the next 30 days from any persons with information that may help solve the disaster. If necessary, 45 days would be allowed. At the end, the board would move to fix blame.

13

On June 18, 1962, the Civil Aeronautics Board issued a report on its investigation into the December 16, 1960 collision between United 826 and TWA 266. The board determined "that the probable cause of this accident was that United Flight 826 proceeded beyond its clearance limit and the confines of the airspace allocated to the flight by air traffic control." The board cited as contributing factors the jet's high rate of speed coupled with a change in routing which shortened their distance to the Preston holding area by about eleven miles. The new clearance and shortened path had "necessitated a rapid descent and maneuvering in order to position the flight at 5,000 feet over Preston...When the clearance was changed, with the subsequent shortcut of approximately 11 nautical miles, the crew apparently made no notation of the shortened time and distance." The report noted the malfunctioning of one of the jet's two navigational receivers further contributed to the problem as the shortcut given to the jet by air traffic control reduced the available time for the crew to retune their single functioning receiver to two ground stations to identify the Preston intersection where they were directed to hold.

The report also concluded that, although their work was not as precise or efficient as it might have been, FAA's traffic controllers on the ground did not violate any regulations. The report took pains to cite a provision of the official manual that a controller was not responsible when pilots failed to heed instructions that would keep them safely separated from other planes. It also concluded that the crash almost certainly could not be attributed to malfunctions of key radio facilities in the area, as inspection of the stations failed to reveal any problems on the day of the crash.

As could be expected, the Air Line Pilots Association was outspokenly critical of the CAB report and its conclusions. The organization issued a statement about six days after the report came out. In it, the association accused the CAB of ignoring air traffic control and other factors in blaming the United plane's crew for the collision. The report was criticized for making no mention of the possibility of an airborne equipment malfunction and for its failure to comment on the obvious lack of coordination and confusion that apparently existed between New York Air Route Traffic Control Center and Idlewild (airport) approach control. Calling for the Board to reconsider its findings on the disaster, the pilots' union called the report a whitewash of the FAA at the expense of the plane crewmen, all killed in the crash.

Charles H. Ruby, president of the pilots' association, said in the statement, "The board's report...ignores what we believe to be a substantial number of highly important contributing factors...We are determined to pursue this case until these factors are made a part of the official report." Ruby said a pilots' accident team that assisted in the crash investigation found a "laxness of air traffic control in the collision," but the CAB ignored these findings, and "completely whitewashes...the FAA's air traffic responsibilities."[73] The 53-year-old Ruby, a National Airlines Pilot, had just replaced Clarence Sayen as President of the Air Line Pilots Association on June 3, 1962.

Capt. Ed Bechtold, eastern regional air safety chairman for the pilots who headed the association's investigation team accused the Board of treating the air traffic control system as if it were infallible. This despite the fact, Bechtold pointed out, that the FAA still made six major rules and systems changes in New York area air traffic control procedures after the accident.

Ruby fiercely defended the United Air Lines crew, saying, "The actions taken by the crew as assumed by the board's report are entirely contrary to those that would be taken by any professional pilot. No crew with the thousands of hours of experience this one had would misuse their navigational equipment in the way the board's report suggests." [74]

    The CAB investigating board, the FAA, and the Pilot's Association representatives all had valid points, and their conclusions were based on each group's own perspective. Although the direct cause of the collision between the two airliners was the failure of the United jet to locate and enter the holding pattern at Preston, many other factors were at play that fateful morning that contributed to the disaster. The Swiss Cheese model of accident causation can be applied to explain what happened not only to cause the airline collision, but the myriad of opportunities the entire system had to prevent it but failed to. This theoretical model is often used in high risk industries such as healthcare, aviation, and nuclear power plants. These types of organizations require a very intense level of risk management because in them, when things go wrong, people die. In this case, the model proposes that between the two airliners, and the collision, there were a variety of barriers in place to prevent a mishap and ensure the safety of the flights from takeoff to landing. Picture these barriers as solid slices of swiss cheese. Each of these barriers, however, has its own latent weaknesses. These weaknesses can be likened to the holes in the cheese slices. These holes are continually varying in size and position in the slices. The philosophy is if you have enough of these layers or barriers, then all of the little holes in the swiss cheese won't actually line up, so you can't get from a scenario to a hazard because there is no clear path through. At any given point, one of the particular barriers will be effective and keep negative consequences from resulting due to a weakness in another barrier. But, at some point, either due to random chance, or deficiencies in one or more of the system barriers, the holes in the slices of cheese will perfectly line up resulting in a "perfect storm" scenario and a tragic accident occurs.

As a result of the accident, the FAA made several changes in regulations to help prevent any repeat of the factors that most likely contributed to the 1960 crash. Special regulation 445 was issued, requiring pilots operating under Instrument Flight Rules to report any in-flight malfunctions of navigational or communication equipment. All turbine-powered aircraft were to be equipped with distance-measuring equipment by January 1, 1963, as were all aircraft of over 12,500 pounds maximum takeoff weight a year later. Radar handoff service was increased to a great extent nationwide. Controllers were also instructed to advise all arriving jets to slow to holding pattern airspeed at least three minutes before arriving at a holding fix. A speed rule was also issued prohibiting aircraft from exceeding 250 knots and 10,000 feet when within 34 miles of a destination airport, except where the safety requirements of tactical military jets required otherwise. New, larger and more widely separated circling areas for planes awaiting their turns to land were put into service across the nation. The FAA directed a tightening of the use of the "radar handoff"—when one controller transfers guidance of a plane to the controller in the next control zone directing that a transfer be made only after the first controller has made sure, over an interphone, that the second controller has identified the proper blip on his radar scope. The FAA also eliminated the "short cut" to Preston as the United jet was routed, instead of down to Robbinsville before the turn northeast onto V123. The V30 routing was eliminated to give pilots more time to re-tune a VHF radio to pick up Preston after making the turn onto V123. Finally, the frequency of the Solberg, NJ VHF aid was changed and the name of the Stroudsburg, PA aid became

Tannersville. These changes were designed to ensure that no pilot could confuse the Solberg and Stroudsburg beams.

In addition, the FAA, in June 1961, commissioned a survey be taken of all near-collisions in the air during a one year period. The survey, completed in August 1962, analyzed more than 2500 near-miss, or near-collision incidents. Although most involved light aircraft and not large commercial airliners, Project Scan pointed out that there was still work to be done in the area of aviation safety. The study recommended an educational program for pilots, improvements in equipment and procedures, and continued collection of anonymous reports "to provide a broad background of information on the near mid-air collision hazard."

In March 1961, in response to the New York airline collision, newly inaugurated President John F. Kennedy, issued an order requesting the FAA to "conduct a scientific, engineering overview of our aviation facilities and related research and development and to prepare a practicable long-range plan to insure efficient and safe control of all air traffic within the United States." A task force called "Project Beacon" was established that would report its findings to the FAA administrator. While the FAA engineers wanted to focus on development of advanced technology to improve the air traffic control system, the air traffic controllers themselves pushed instead for the modernization and improvement of existing technology. They felt there was a pressing need for more immediate fixes and a reluctance to wait for more modern technology to be developed in an unknown period of time in the future. The final recommendations of the Project Beacon task force agreed more strongly with the controllers than the engineers, concluding that an improved radar system would be the primary tool for air traffic control for at least the next decade. Whereas previously controllers kept track of airplanes on the radar screen with flight strips, plastic markers ("shrimp boats"), and grease-penciled markings on the radar screen, the system would now be upgraded to display altitude and identification visually in alphanumeric characters on the radar screen. The amount of controller workload would thus be reduced and help eliminate much of the confusion in air traffic control.

The roll-out of the changes to the air traffic control system as result of Project Beacon did not go as planned. It was clear that there was a large difference between the promised improvements and what the system could actually do and that the project participants grossly underestimated the technical problems inherent in the task. To make matters worse, the funds needed for the improvements would not be forthcoming as, instead of more money to make the changes, the FAA saw budget cuts through the 1960s. Four years after the Project Beacon recommendations were made, many controllers were still using the old manual "shrimp boat" system despite the fact that air traffic growth had jumped over 75% since the early 60's. By the late 1960's the air traffic control system was once again in disarray.

The collision of United Flight 826 and TWA 266 was, at the time it occurred, the deadliest aircraft accident in history. It remained so until May 12, 1968 when a U.S. Air Force Lockheed C-130 Hercules was shot down over Kham Duc, South Vietnam killing all 155 people on board-- mostly South Vietnamese civilians being evacuated. The following year saw the Park Slope crash surpassed as the worst commercial aviation disaster when Viasa Airline Flight 742 from Caracas, Venezuela to Miami, Florida crashed when it hit some power lines on take-off. Eight-four people on board and 71 on the ground—a total of 155 people-- were killed.

The intersection of 7th Avenue and Sterling Place today shows the tell-tale scars of the disaster that shook the Brooklyn neighborhood almost 60 years ago. The building at 126 Sterling Place, where a portion of the United jet's left wing had been embedded in the roof, still stands but its bunting-patterned tin cornice is gone. The first dozen sections of brick below the rebuilt roof don't match the rest. They are shinier, lighter, newer. In the back of the brownstone at 20 7th Avenue, a second-floor window was never replaced and was bricked over. Residents still claim to be finding pieces of the plane in their backyards to this day. Over forty years after the crash, Park Slope resident Steve Keltner was walking by the vacant lot where the Pillar of Fire Church had once been when he spotted a piece of metal, charred and chalky, protruding from the ground. It was a twisted piece of aluminum, about a foot long, with rounded holes cut in it. Investigators from the National Transportation Safety Board confirmed after viewing photos that the relic appeared to be an aircraft part. Keltner found two other aircraft pieces, one about three feet high, crimped at one end, the other about five feet by three feet with a diagonal pattern of rivets and holes running along the side. This piece bore a rectangular black tag: "No. 5 main tank Auxiliary Fuel. Structural limit 17,605 lbs." Officials at Boeing, which acquired the DC-8's manufacturer, McDonnell Douglas, said that the piece appeared to be part of the right wing of a DC-8. The relics are apparently Mr. Keltner's to keep. The Civil Aeronautics Board, which guarded and cataloged the remains of the jet, no longer exists, and its successor agency, the National Transportation Safety Board, does not intend to reopen the case. "The N.T.S.B. has no interest whatsoever in the preservation or possession of such wreckage," said a spokesman, Peter Knudson. [75]

Located in Greenwood Heights, Brooklyn, Green-Wood Cemetery lies several blocks southwest of Prospect Park, between Park Slope, Windsor Terrace, Borough Park, Kensington, and Sunset Park.

It was an era before DNA identifications were possible, and United Airlines had to decide what to do with the partial human remains that were unidentifiable from the 1960 crash. On January 5, 1961, United purchased a grave lot—number 38325—in the Green-Wood Cemetery. Three caskets of "Fragmentary Human Remains" were filled from the Park Slope crash site and were buried there. No marker was placed on the grave.

Fifty years later, the staff of the Green-Wood Cemetery decided it would be fitting to design and erect a memorial to all those who died as a result of the tragedy of the United/TWA collision. The memorial, designed by Superintendent of the Grounds, Art Presson, and other Green-Wood staff, features a grove of one hundred Quaking Aspen trees, alcoves, benches, and a path, on a slope adjoining lot 38325. An eight-foot inscribed granite monument, designed by Vice President for Operations, Ken Taylor, was erected.

On Thursday, December 16, 2010, the 50th anniversary of this deadly crash, at 10:00 a.m., Green-Wood dedicated the memorial, as the Sanitation Department's bagpipers played "Amazing Grace." Sanitation worker Charles Cooper was one of the six victims on the ground who perished. The granite monument was unveiled by Brooklyn Borough President Mary Markowitz and City Councilman Vincent Gentile. The ceremony was attended by many who were at the scene of the crash fifty years ago, as well as some of the family members of the victims. About 100 people including family members of several of the victims attended the ceremony. They shared their stories and their grief, only slightly numbed by the passage of time.

In a touching moment, a letter was read before a moment of silence. The letter was written by Randee and William Baltz, the younger siblings of Stephen Baltz, who for a short time was the lone crash survivor.

"He was 11 years old at the time, and terribly burned and broken. But, when my father first came to his bedside at the hospital, Steve smiled and said to him, 'Next time I fly, I want my own plane. I want to be the pilot.' He was already looking to the future and never gave up hope."

Kevin Root's parents, Florence and Samuel, were on the United Flight. He was only five years old when they were killed, coming home from a vacation in Las Vegas. Root teared up during the ceremony. "This was a long time coming," he said.   "I thought I was over it, but you never get over it. It's unending."

List of Passengers who died in "Park Slope Crash"

United Airlines, Flight 826, Passengers:

Alexander, Ruth, 44, Butte, Montana. Nurse and student at University of Utah, Salt Lake City, working toward her bachelor's degree in nursing education.

Baltz, Steven, 11, Wilmette, Illinois.

Bock, Albert, Holden, Massachusetts. Superintendent of Midwestern operations of Wyman-Gorman Co. makers of airplane landing gear and wing struts for the government.

Bowen, Lowell L, 35, San Francisco, California. Bechtol Corporation.

Braun, Allen E.

Braun, Mario, Barrilaco, Mexico

Bruner, Henry C. "Hank," 36, Stamford, Connecticut. Staff manager of marketing and sales for Johns-Manville Pipe Division.

Bustos, Enrique, 28, New York City, New York. On his way home after visiting a sister in Evanston, Illinois.

Butler, Hugh S., 50, New York City, New York. Executive vice president of the Simmons Mattress Co.

Capri, George, 55, Las Vegas, Nevada. Formerly part owner of the Flamingo Hotel.

Dileo, Frank R., 21, Long Island New York. Senior at University of Utah.

Dotzenroth, Paul, 36, Wayzata, Minnesota. President of Baker Engineering Corp., in St Louis Park.

Drayton, Walter C., 36, Summit New Jersey. General sales manager for Bolco Brass & Copper company in Newark, NJ.

Dumalski, Edwige, 40, Oak Lawn Illinois. Clerk with United Airlines.

Dumalski, Joelle,11, Oak Lawn Illinois. Daughter of Mrs. Edwige Dumalski.

Dumalski, Patrick, 14, Oak Lawn Illinois. Son of Mrs. Edwige Dumalski.

Emery, Thomas, Tulsa Oklahoma

Enklaar, Fritz. H; New York City, New York

Freese, Donald, 27, Seattle, Washington. Reservations agent with United Airlines Seattle office.

Garamendi, Ricardo, 27, Winnemucca Nevada. Shepherd.

Gielessen, E., originated at New York

Gordon, Susan, 18, New York City, New York. Freshman, University of Wisconsin

Hodgkins, Anne, 22, New Canaan, Connecticut. Sophomore at Barat College Lake Forest, IL.

Hotinski, Michael, 40, Staten Island, New York. Sales Associate, R. Hoe and company.

Jenks, Stephen M., 17, New York City, New York. Freshman at University of Chicago.

Kamlet, Dr. Jonas. New York City, New York.

Katz, Samuel R. 19, Cambria Heights, New York. Seaman 2 class U.S. Navy

Keenan, George, 32, Latham New York. Engineer with General Electric's installation and service department.

Korey, Sidney, 57, Chicago, Illinois. Owner of Chicago Laundry and Cleaners Supply Company.

Kosturn, Howard, 40, Wilmette, Illinois. Midwest sales manager for the BVD company, Inc., hosiery division, of New York City.

LaRiviere, Peggy, Greenwich, Connecticut. Freshman at Barat College.

Lee, Ardythe Ann, 21, Des Moines, Iowa. Employee of Northwestern Bell Telephone Co.

Leigh, Stuart, 38, New Vernon New Jersey. Employed with Garwood firm, Thatcher Furnace Co

Lopez, Michael, 20, Hampstead New York. Junior at Northwestern University.

Loughran, Thomas, 24, Chicago, Illinois. Salesman for Standard & Poor's corporation, business reporting service.

Mallory, Darnell, 19, Summit, New Jersey. Freshman, Omaha University.

Martin, Annette., 32, Chicago, Illinois. Private secretary at Ilg Ventilating Company in Chicago.

McCauliffe, Robert, 36, Paxton, Massachusetts. Sales engineer for the Reynolds wire division of National Standard Company.

McHugh, John, Long Island New York. Employed with Amplex corporation

Miner, Dorothy, 27, Chicago, Illinois. Head nurse at University of Illinois Hospital, Chicago.

Mogren, Lester, 36, Wappingers Falls, New York. Associate product field engineer for IBM.

Mountain, James, 20, Mount Kisco, New York. Sophomore, Iowa State University student.

Mueller, Herman, New York City, with Liquidometer Corp.

Olsen, Thor, 45, Downers Grove, Illinois.

Pandolfini, Joseph, 19., White Plains New York. Student, Colorado State University.

Parker, Edna H., San Francisco, California.

Parks, Beverly, 22, San Francisco, California. Former employee of Pacific Southwest Airlines.

Pentti, Aarne Samuel. Finland. Reservation originated in Tampa FL

Petzold, Lawrence.C., 35, Sayerville, New Jersey. Technical service manager of the Hercules Powder Co. in Parlin NJ.

Platt, Elsie, 61, Barrington Illinois. Flying to New York to be with her daughter who had just had a baby.

Plummer, David, 36, Fishkill New York. Systems technician at IBM in Poughkeepsie.

Post, Catherine, 18, Pleasantville New York. Freshman at the Medill School of Journalism Northwestern University.

Reames, Earl, H., 41, Port Chester New York. Chief mate of the steamship Steel Recorder, in Seattle, Washington.

Richmond, Harold T.A., 44, Bronxville New York. President of the Custom-Made Paper Bag Company in Long Island City, Queens,

Riley, Earle F., 44, Bremerton Washington. A manager of Lent's Inc., in Bremerton was en route to his father's funeral in Rhode Island.

Root, Samuel, 34, Freeport, New York. Executive with the North Shore Sports Wear Company in Glen Cove, L.I.

Root, Florence, 32, Freeport, New York. Wife of Samuel Root.

Rosenfield, Jonas, Roslyn New York. Student, University of Wisconsin in Madison.

Ryan, Thomas, 38, Pelham New York. Executive V-P Mechanical Contractors Association of America.

Salkin, Morton, New York City, New York.

Saxon, Elliott. Employed with Cookerama, New York City.

Schierer, Thomas J., 45, Trenton New Jersey. Employee of Reichold Chemicals, Inc. in Elizabeth.

Scholz, E. Bernard, New York City, New York.

Schuelke, Arthur F. 47, Ossining, New York. General Manager of three trade magazines for Reuben H. Donnelly Corp.

Sokolosky, Alvin, 34, Baltimore Maryland. Executive producer for the Bert Claster Enterprises, producer of television shows.

Sommers, Charles E., Watertown, Connecticut. Vice president of General Time Corp. New York.

Sullivan, George D. Jr., 34, Bronx, New York.

Tiska, Theodora, Greenwich, Connecticut. Junior at Rosary College, River Forest, IL.

Tuttle, John N., Montvalle, New Jersey. Eastern regional manager for Nesbitt Fruit Products, Inc. of Los Angeles.

Vanwyck, George B., New York City, New York. Senior methods engineer in the merchandising department of the Johns-Manville Corp in New York City.

Wheeler, John Paul, 20, Taunton, Massachusetts. Airman 2 class, U.S. Air Force based at Offutt Air Force Base.

Winniger, S. Edward, New York City, New York. President of Nicholson Company and Winiger Company, New York City.

Wittmer, Carlos Jose, 22, Caracas, Venezuela. Graduated from Industrial Engineering College in Chicago and returning home to Venezuela.

Wittmer, Olga, 18, Caracas, Venezuela

Wittmer, Carlos Jr (infant of Carlos and Olga Wittmer)

Woodward, Rebecca, 18, Dobbs Ferry, New York. Student, University of Utah.

United Air Lines, Flight 826, Crew:

Bouthan, Ann Marie, 29, stewardess, Los Angeles, California.

Ferrar, Augustine Louise, 25, stewardess, Manhattan Beach California.

Fiebing, Robert W., 40, first officer, Woodland Hills, California.

Keller, Patricia Ann, 23, stewardess, Hawthorne, California.

Mahoney, Mary F. 24, stewardess, Manhattan Beach California.

Prewitt, Richard Eugene (Gene), 30, flight engineer, Torrance, California

Sawyer, Robert H., 46, Hemet California

TWA, Flight 266, Passengers

Bitters, Richard "Dick" L., 33, Athens, Ohio. Assistant to Dr. John C. Baker, Ohio University president and associate director of the Ohio University Fund.

Bricker, Louella, 36, London, Ohio. Mother of four she was en route to Boston to take her 7-year-old son, George home for the holidays from a school for the blind.

Briggs, Nancy, 19, Springfield, Massachusetts. Junior, Ohio State University.

Buchheit, Jack, 30, Wooster, Ohio. National executive secretary of Pi Lamda Phi fraternity.

Burten, Arthur, 35, Newark, New Jersey. Industrial sales manager at Astron Corp, East Newark.

Chandler, Arthur W., 21, New Ipswich, New Hampshire. Airman second class, U.S. Air Force, stationed at Lockbourne AFB, Columbus OH with the 366th Organizational Maintenance Squadron.

Clothier, C., New York. With Sperry Corp.

Connell, Robert, 24, Columbus, Ohio. Ohio State University graduate student.

Dahlberg A, New York. Representative of the American Fire Insurance Company

Ellis, Robert., 29, Scarsdale, New York; Member of the Benton & Bowles advertising firm as assistant producer of radio-TV commercials for the agency.

Evans, David, 21, Charden, Ohio. Senior, Ohio State University. Fraternity brother of Richard Magnuson, who also died in the crash.

Ewart, Cyril. G. 49, Columbus, Ohio. Vice President of "Highlights for Children" magazine.

Fisher, John H., 55, Scotch Plains, New Jersey. Vice president in charge of engineering at Astron Corp, East Newark.

Flood, Vincent, 29, South Orange, New Jersey. Dominican Novice in the seminary at St. Joseph's Priory in Somerset, Ohio.

Gingold, Alex., 45, Columbus, Ohio. District salesman for Rugby Knitting Mills, Buffalo, NY.

Griebel, Peter, 24, Hilliard, Ohio. Fuller Brush salesman en route to Newton CT to visit family.

Griebel, Karen, 22, Hilliard, Ohio. Wife of Pater Griebel

Griebel, Jennifer, 3 weeks old, Hilliard, Ohio. Infant daughter of Peter and Jennifer Griebel.

Helton, Carter B., 60, Dayton, Ohio. Owner and operator of Helton Travel Service in Dayton. He was en route to Boston to the bedside of his 19-year-old son Michael a student at Babson Institute,

Wellesley Mass. who was being treated for tuberculosis at a Boston hospital.

Horsey, James M., 30, Front Royal, Virginia. Product sales manager of the Riverton (VA) Lima and Coal Co.

Israel, Esta, 40, New York City, New York. Representative of the American Photo Corp.

Krumm, Albert, 40, Columbus Ohio. Attorney, vice president, general counsel and member of the board of directors of the Franklin Federal Savings and Loan Co.

Magnuson, Richard, 21, Hartford, Connecticut. Student, Ohio State University and president of the Tau Kappa Epsilon Fraternity at Ohio State.

McEachern, Robert, 22, Cass City, Michigan. First year law student at Ohio State University.

Mullins, Cecil W., Dayton, Ohio. Operator of the Mastercraft, Co., an aluminum storm sash firm. En route to visit his wife's parents in Puerto Rico.

Mullins, Juanita, Dayton, Ohio. Wife of Cecil Mullins.

Tracy Mullins, 3 months old, Dayton, Ohio. Daughter of Cecil and Juanita Mullins.

Myers, Garry C Jr.., Columbus Ohio. Publisher of the magazine "Highlights for Children", and president of the Grandview Heights Board of Education.

Myers, Mary, 38, Co-editor of Highlights for Children.

Petersen, Warren, 43, Baldwin, New York. Power plant staff engineer for the Republic Aircraft Co.

Rapkin, Thomas D., 31, Toronto Ontario. Director of community service awards for radio station WVKO, Columbus and completing pre-graduate work at the Ohio State University.

Simpson, Robert, 57, New Milford, New Jersey. Bendix Corp, Teterboro, NJ

Swenson, Arthur B., 42, Glastonbury, Connecticut. Project engineer of the Pratt-Whitney Aircraft Corp. of East Hartford CT. He had been attending business sessions at Wright-Patterson Air Force Base.

Tierney, Edward, 34, West Carrollton, Ohio. Textile engineer for the Dayton Rubber Co.

Voelker, Edward H., 87. Returning home from a visit with his son in Columbus.

Walden, John S., 42, Greenwich, Connecticut. Salesman for West Virginia Pulp and Paper Co.

Walsh, Raymond J., 43, Middleton, Connecticut. President of Wesleyan University Press, Columbus.

Watman, Dr. Robert, 43, Columbus, Ohio. Associate Professor of surgery at University Hospital, Columbus.

Wright, Murray T., 30, North Ferrisburg, Vermont. Specialist in General Electric missile development was returning from Wright-Patterson AFB Dayton to the Burlington, VT plant.

TWA Flight 266 Crew

Bowen, Dean, 32, first officer, Glen Cove, New York

Gernat, Margaret, 24, stewardess, New York City, New York.

Post, Patricia A., 21, stewardess, Jackson Heights, New York.

Rosenthal, Leroy L., 30, flight engineer, New Hyde Park, New York

Wollam, David A., 39, Captain, Little Neck Road, Huntington, New York.

Memorial to the victims of the collision of United 826 and TWA 266. Green-Wood Cemetery, Brooklyn.

Photo by Tim Azzara

IN MEMORY OF THOSE WHO PERISHED
IN THE SKY AND ON THE GROUND
IN THE MID-AIR COLLISION OF
TWA FLIGHT 266 AND
UNITED AIRLINES FLIGHT 826
OVER NEW YORK CITY
ON DECEMBER 16, 1960.

THE DEADLIEST AIRLINE DISASTER
IN AMERICAN HISTORY AT THE TIME,
IT CLAIMED 134 VICTIMS.

THIRTY-NINE PASSENGERS
AND FIVE CREW MEMBERS
DIED ON TWA FLIGHT 266.

SEVENTY-SEVEN PASSENGERS,
SEVEN CREW MEMBERS
AND SIX PERSONS ON
THE GROUND LOST THEIR LIVES
IN THE CRASH OF
UNITED AIRLINES FLIGHT 826.

THE TWA AIRLINER FELL TO THE GROUND
IN MILLER FIELD ON STATEN ISLAND.

THE UNITED FLIGHT CRASHED
AT THE INTERSECTION
OF SEVENTH AVENUE
AND STERLING PLACE
IN PARK SLOPE, BROOKLYN.

THE REMAINS OF
THE UNIDENTIFIED VICTIMS
REST NEARBY IN LOT 38325
GRAVE 980.

Memorial to the victims of the collision of United 826 and TWA 266, Green-Wood Cemetery, Brooklyn.

Photo by Tim Azzara

Grave marker at the site of the interment of the unidentified fragmentary remains from the crash. Green-Wood Cemetery, Brooklyn.

Photo by Tim Azzara

The building at 126 Sterling Place, where a portion of the United jet's left wing had been embedded in the roof, still stands but its bunting-patterned tin cornice is gone. The first dozen sections of brick below the rebuilt roof don't match the rest.

Photo by Tim Azzara

7th Avenue looking south, the intersection is where the tail section of the United jet came to rest.

Photo by Tim Azzara

COLLISION ANGLE
(as per official accident report)

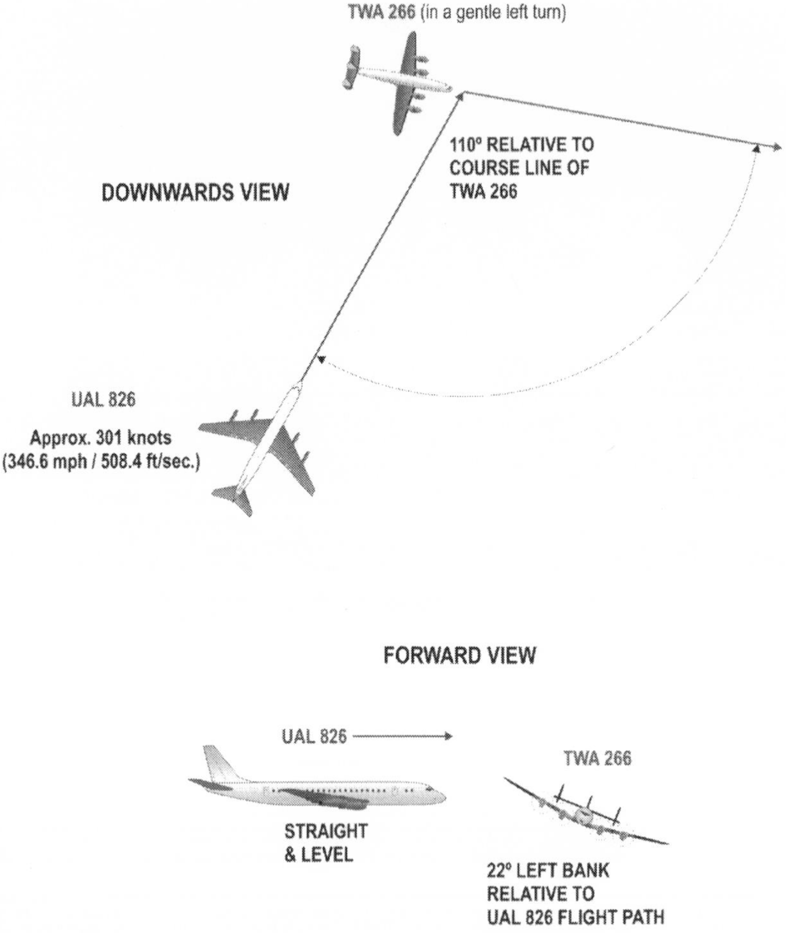

TWA 266 (in a gentle left turn)

110° RELATIVE TO
COURSE LINE OF
TWA 266

DOWNWARDS VIEW

UAL 826

**Approx. 301 knots
(346.6 mph / 508.4 ft/sec.)**

FORWARD VIEW

UAL 826 →

TWA 266

**STRAIGHT
& LEVEL**

**22° LEFT BANK
RELATIVE TO
UAL 826 FLIGHT PATH**

Diagram showing the angle of collision between United 826 and TWA 266.

By Louis Gonzalez

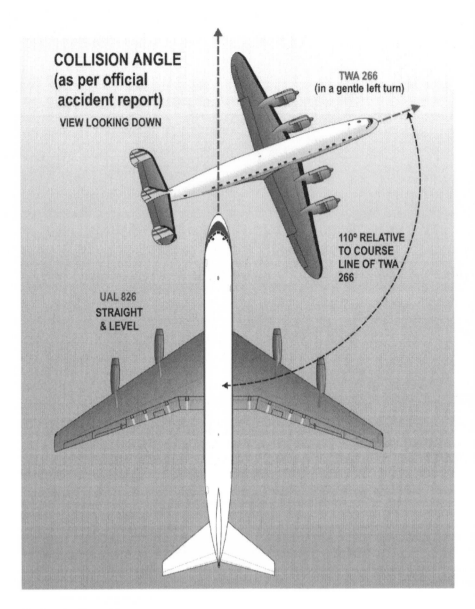

By Louis Gonzalez

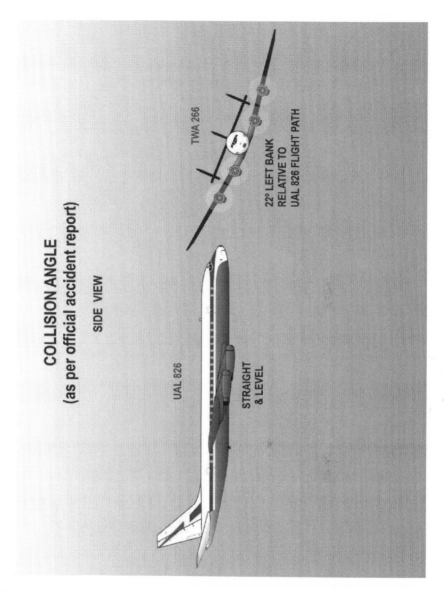

By Louis Gonzalez

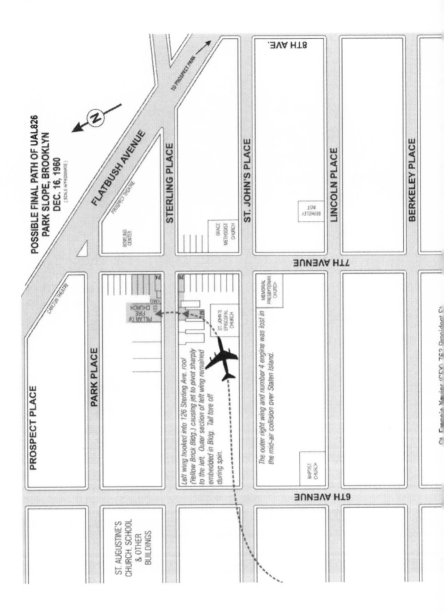

Diagram of Park Slope neighborhood showing the possible flight path of the United jet as it came down.

By Louis Gonzelez

John Marotta's diagram of his recollection of the scene at Sterling Place and 7th Avenue at the time of the crash of the United jet.

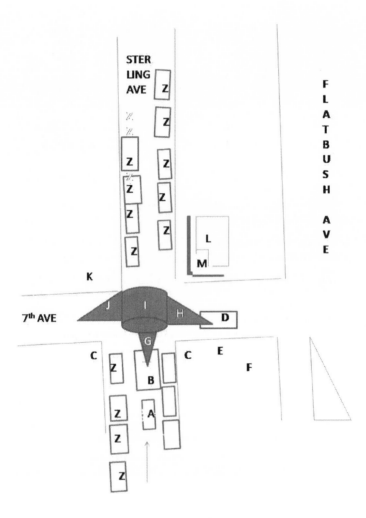

LEGEND

a) **Sterling Ave was a one way street going in the position at the bottom**

b) Z were the parked cars on both sides of the street there wasn't any room to turn around actually just enough room to open the doors.
c) A was the car I was in with my friend who was driving.
d) B was the truck in front of us stopped at a Stop Sign.
e) C where the Stop Signs were.
f) D was the car that was trapped under the Tail Wing (H). The plane (what was left of it) was leaning to the right I and J).
g) G has the upright Tail of the plan leaning backwards on the top of the truck B.
h) E was the buried hydrant (covered with snow from a city Snow Plow). We had to find it for the Fire Dept and dig it out by hand.
i) F was the Bowling Alley that was used for first aid and later in the day as a temporary morgue and also a Red Cross location for Coffee and donuts.
j) K was a corner building, during the entire day I never got on that side of the plane but I saw an older woman on the ledge – to this day I'm not sure of what I saw – but she was like an angel.
k) L was a brownstone M was the concrete front yard and the black line represents the fence that surrounded it. It was typical of the type and style of the time it was built. It was concrete, about two feet high and the top was lined with wrought iron spikes. It was the cause of many injuries.

By John Marotta

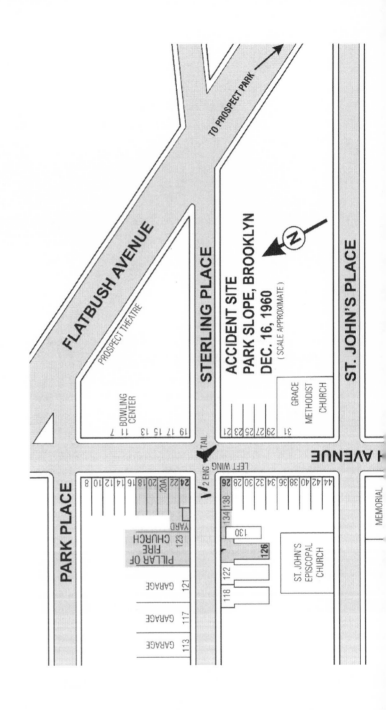

Site of the United jet crash in the Park Slope section of Brooklyn

By Louis Gonzalez

Endnotes

[1] John Bronwlee, "What It Was Really Like to Fly During the Golden Age of Travel" https://www.fastcodesign.com/3022215/what-it-was-really-like-to-fly-during-the-golden-age-of-travel

[2] Thomas Pugh and Neal Patterson, "Crash Pilot Rated Over Average," Daily News [New York] Jan 11, 1961

[3] "College Girl Had No Fear of Death" The Courier News, Salt Lake City, Utah Dec 17, 196

[4] "I Love You All So Much" Democrat and Chronicle, Jan 15, 1961

[5] Doris Fortune, "Tragic Plane Crashes Bring Grief to County," Fort Lauderdale News Dec 18, 1960

[6] Bob Wright, "A Monday Would Have Been Worse," Daily News Staff Writer, Dayton Daily News, Dec 17, 1960

[7] "20 Ohioans Among 135 Who Died in Collision of Airliners," The Sandusky Register Dec 17, 1960

[8] Ibid

[9] "Sees Pilot Pal in Columbus, O., Prior to Crash," The Kansas City Times Dec 17, 1960

[10] "20 Ohioans Among 135 Who Died in Collision of Airliners," The Sandusky Register, Dec 17, 1960

[11] Joseph A. McCartin, "Collision Course: Ronald Reagan, the Air Traffic Controllers, and the Strike, Oxford University Press, New York, 2011

[12] Thomas Pugh and Henry Lee, "10 Who Saw Air Crash Tell All, and Little," Daily News [New York] Jan 5, 1961

[13] Charles Grutzner, "Crash Witnesses Describe Destruction on Ground," New York Times, Dec 17, 1960

[14] Henry Machirella and Eugene Spagnole, "Horror in the Air as Witnesses Saw It," Daily News [New York], Dec 17, 1960

[15] Grutzner, op. cit.

[16] Thomas Buckley, "SI Homes Spared By Falling Debris," New York Times, Dec 17, 1960

[17] Ibid

[18] Joseph Kiernan, Edward Kirkman, and Henry Lee, "133 Dead in Airliners

Crash, 6 of them in Brooklyn Streets," Daily News [New York] Dec 17, 1960
[19] Machirella and Spagnole, op. cit.
[20] Edward V. McCarthy, "Tragedy Portrait," The Courier Journal, Dec 25, 1960
[21] J. David Goodman, "Park Slope Plane Crash: The Constellation Comes Down," Dec 16, 2010. https://cityroom.blogs.nytimes.com/tag/park-slope-plane-crash/?_R=0
[22] "Air tragedy history's worst; toll rises," The Tennessean, Dec 17, 1960
[23] Clarence Dean, "Brooklyn Scene: A Quiet Byway Is Invaded by Death and Chaos," New York Times, Dec 17, 1960
[24] Ibid
[25] Robert McCarthy and Robert Walsh, "Hunt Residents Amidst Debris in Death Alley," Daily News [New York], Dec 17, 1960
[26] "125 Lives Lost as Airliners Collide Over New York," Des Moines Tribune, Dec 16, 1960
[27] Dean, op. cit.
[28] Pugh and Lee, op. cit.
[29] "Keuka Student Describes Horror at Brooklyn Air Crash," Democrat and Chronicle, Jan 8, 1961
[30] Stories of Fire by Paul Hashagen, Fire Books, New York, 2017
[31] Ibid
[32] Ibid
[33] Nathaniel Altman, "Pillar of Fire: Interview with Dorothy M. Fletcher," Park Slope Reader, https://web.archive.org/web/20041015121156/http://psreader.com:80/article45.html
[34] "Tiny Boy, Only Crash Survivor, Loses Battle for Life in New York," Reno Gazette Journal, Dec 17, 1960
[35] Altman, op. cit. I
[36] Jack Mallon and Theo Wilson, "Burned, Dazed, Lad Came Thru," Daily News [New York], Dec 16, 1960
[37] "Mother in Tears Learns Her Son Survived Crash," Hartford Courant, Dec 17 1960
[38] Vincent Butler, "Fate Chooses 1 of 127 to Live," Chicago Tribune, Dec 17, 1960
[39] Ibid
[40] Emily S. Rueb, "Park Slope Plane Crash, Voices of Those Who Were There," https://cityroom.blogs.nytimes.com/tag/park-slope-plane-crash/?_r=0

[41] Robert McCarthy, "Mom and Dad Lose Their Stevie And the City Shares Their Grief," Daily News [New York], Dec 18, 1960

[42] Emanuel Perlmutter, "Boy Who Survived Crash Dies; 'Stevie Tried Hard,' Father says," New York Times, Dec 18, 1960

[43] Fred Ferguson, "'Stevie 'Closed His Eyes and Went to Sleep'" Fort Lauderdale News, Dec 19 1960

[44] Joseph Egelhof, "Sole Survivor of Crash Dies," Chicago Tribune Press Service, Chicago Tribune, Dec 18, 1960

[45] "Bride, Parents, Kin Wait, Then—Heartbreak!" Chicago Tribune, December 17, 1960

[46] Gay Telese, "Air Crash Fading Into Thing of Past," New York Times, Jan 1, 1961

[47] "2 Youngsters Share Grief of Baltz Family," Chicago Tribune, Dec 23, 1960

[48] "Crash Victim Steven Buried in Snowy Plot," Chicago Tribune, Dec 21, 1960

[49] Russell Porter, "A Pilot Off Route, U.S. Officials Hint," New York Times, Dec 17, 1960

[50] Ibid

[51] Relman Morin, "Tragedy, Disputed Allegations, Probe Mark Worst Air Accident in History," Daily Press, Dec 25, 1960

[52] Edward Hudson, "Quesada Asserts Signals Worked," New York Times, Dec 22, 1960

[53] "Quesada Says Jet Failed to Ask Aid," New York Times, January 2, 1961

[54] Richard Witkin, "Hearing Opening on Air Collision," New York Times, Jan 4, 1961

[55] Thomas Pugh, "U.S. to Open Air Disaster Hearings," Daily News [New York] ,Jan 4, 1961

[56] Thomas Pugh and Henry Lee, "Try to Show FAA Let Jet Stray Into Disaster," Daily News [New York], Jan 6, 1961

[57] Ibid

[58] Ibid

[59] Thomas Pugh, "Also Led Astray Say 4 Disaster Pilots," Daily News ,Jan 7, 1961

[60] "Testimony in Air Crash Conflicts on Radio Aid by Associated Press," The Salt Lake Tribune, Jan 7, 1961

[61] "3 Pilots Testify Radio Aid Faulty On Day of Crash by New York Herald Tribune," The Miami News, Jan 7, 1961

[62] Richard Witkin, "Pilots Tell CAB of Radio Trouble," New York Times, Jan 7, 1961

[63] Albert Sehlstedt, Jr. "Pilots Testify on Troubles With Beacon on Crash Day," The Baltimore Sun, Jan 7, 1961

[64] "3 Pilots Testify Radio Aid Faulty On Day of Crash," by New York Herald Tribune, The Miami News, Jan 7, 1961

[65] Wayne Thomis, "Radar Termed Skimpy in NY Air Collision," Chicago Tribune, Jan 11, 1961

[66] Ibid

[67] Richard Witkin, "FAA Will Check Jet Flight Safety," New York Times, Jan 12, 1961

[68] Thomas Pugh, "No More Short Cuts, Crash Probers Told," Daily News [New York], Jan 12, 1961

[69] Thomas Pugh, "Plane Collision Seen on Radar at LaGuardia," Daily News [New York], Jan 13, 1961

[70] "Crash Pilot Alerted, Quiz Told," Detroit Free Press, Jan 13, 1961.

[71] Thomas Pugh, "Plane Collision Seen on Radar at LaGuardia," Daily News, [New York] Jan 13, 1961

[72] Wayne Thomis, "United Puts NY Air Crash Blame on FAA," Chicago Tribune, Jan 14 1961

[73] "CABs Report On Crash Hit," The Baltimore Sun, Jun 25, 1962

[74] Ibid

[75] Andy Newman, "Park Slope Plane Crash | Scarred Roofs and Jet Parts," Dec 15, 2010 https://cityroom.blogs.nytimes.com/2010/12/15/park-slope-plane-crash-the-lingering-scars/#more-254839

Made in the USA
Middletown, DE
18 December 2022

19203663R00090